advancing learning, changing lives

Get ready for...

Edexcel GCSE
History

Jane Shuter   Steve Waugh
Series editor: Angela Leonard

D0178374

9112000019 4959

A PEARSON COMPANY

Published by Pearson Education Limited, a company incorporated in
England and Wales, having its registered office at Edinburgh Gate,
Harlow, Essex, CM20 2JE. Registered company number: 872828
www.pearsonschoolsandfecolleges.co.uk
Edexcel is a registered trademark of Edexcel Limited
Text © Pearson Education Limited 2011
First published 2011
12 11 10
10 9 8 7 6 5 4 3 2 1
British Library Cataloguing in Publication Data
A catalogue record for this book is available from the British Library
ISBN 978 1 846909 57 3

Copyright notice

Designed and typeset by Jerry Udall
Cover image: Mary Evans Picture Library/ Met Police Authority
Printed in Italy by Rotolito Lombarda

Disclaimer

This material has been published on behalf of Edexcel and offers high-quality support for the delivery
of Edexcel qualifications. This does not mean that the material is essential to achieve any Edexcel
qualification, nor does it mean that it is the only suitable material available to support any Edexcel
qualification. Edexcel material will not be used verbatim in setting any Edexcel examination or
assessment. Any resource lists produced by Edexcel shall include this and other appropriate resources.
Copies of official specifications for all Edexcel qualifications may be found on the Edexcel website:
www.edexcel.com

Acknowledgements

The publisher would like to thank the following for their kind permission to reproduce:

Photographs:

(Key: b-bottom; c-centre; l-left; r-right; t-top)

p.6l Alamy / Mary Evans Picture Library, p6r Topfoto; p.7tl Alamy / Pictorial Press Ltd, p.7tr Topfoto / Museum of London / HIP, p.7bl Alamy / Jochen Tack; p7br Imperial War Museum; p.9 Alamy / LordPrice Collection; p.10 Alamy / Pictorial Press Ltd; p.12 Alamy / Mary Evans Picture Library; p.13 PA / PA Archive; p.15 Getty / Hulton Archive; p.17 Alamy / Pictorial Press Ltd; p.18 Alamy / Mary Evans Picture Library; p.22 Topfoto; p.24 Getty Images / Hulton Archive; p.25 ITN source/ Gaumont British newsreel (Reuters); p.26 NI Syndication; p.28 Topfoto; p.29 Topfoto; p.30 Getty / AFP; p.31 Alamy/Trinity Mirror/ Mirrorpix; p.35 Alamy / Pictorial Press Ltd; p.37 Alamy / Mary Evans Picture Library; p.38 Alamy / Jochen Tack; p.41 Topfoto / Topham PicturePoint; p.44 Imperial War Museum; p.47 Topfoto / Museum of London / HIP; p.48 Alamy / Mary Evans Picture Library; p.52 Getty/ Time Life Pictures/ George Rodger; p.56 Alamy / Trinity Mirror / Mirrorpix; p.57 University of Kent / Express Syndication; p.59l Getty / Popperfoto; p.59r University of Kent / Solo Syndication; p.65 Imperial War Museum; p.66 Mary Evans Picture Library / Illustrated London News; p.68 Imperial War Museum; p.74 University of Kent / Solo Syndication; p.82 Corbis / Hulton-Deutsch Collection; p.85 Alamy / INTERFOTO

All other images © Pearson Education

Written Sources:

p.18 Sources B and D Reproduced with permission of Curtis Brown Group Ltd, London on behalf of the Trustees of the Mass Observation Archive Copyright © The Trustees of the Mass Observation Archive; p.22 Source B © The National Archives http://www.nationalarchives.gov.uk/cabinetpapers/alevelstudies/origins-nhs.htm as on 6/4/11; p.22 Source C compiled from Table 11.2, *British Social Trends Since 1900*, ed A. H. Halsey, Macmillan Press Ltd, 1988; p.23 Source D compiled from Tables 11.36 and 11.37, *British Social Trends Since 1900*, ed A. H. Halsey, Macmillan Press Ltd, 1988; p.37 Source A from *British Social Trends Since 1900*, ed A. H. Halsey, Macmillan Press Ltd, 1988; p.38 Source C compiled from *British Social Trends Since 1900*, ed A. H. Halsey, Macmillan Press Ltd, 1988 and National Statistics online; p.51 Source B © Telegraph Media Group Limited 1940; p.55 Source B © British Medical Journal; p.58 Source A © Evening Standard; Source C p.59 Crown Copyright; p.61 Source F *The World at War 1938-45*, S. Waugh & J. Wright, © 2007, Hodder Education. Reproduced by Permission of Hodder Education; p.81 Source B Martin Gilbert, author of *The Holocaust: The Jewish Tragedy*, Fontana edition, HarperCollins; p.84 Source F Martin Gilbert, author of *The Holocaust: The Jewish Tragedy*, Fontana edition, HarperCollins; Miriam Novitch Collection.

Every effort has been made to trace the copyright holders and we apologise in advance for any unintentional omissions. We would be pleased to insert the appropriate acknowledgement in any subsequent edition of this publication.

Contents

Thinking about history

Historical skills

6

Studying history is about asking questions. To answer these questions you learn a set of skills that help you uncover things about the past such as the reasons for, effects of and importance of different events.

What were the effects of bombing raids like this one in London during the Second World War?

Causation

When you ask why something happened, you are thinking about causation – what caused something to happen. Learning how to deal with causation questions helps you to understand the past and modern life too.

Consequence

When you ask what effects something had, you are thinking about consequence. Events usually have more than one consequence. This bombing of London by German planes during the Second World War (above) destroyed homes and caused distress. It also made the British people more determined to win the war.

Why was this woman treated like this?

Helping hand

One of the most important things to remember in your study of history is that you need to use information to answer questions. When you answer questions:

- give useful, relevant, detail in your answers wherever you can
- explain your reasoning.

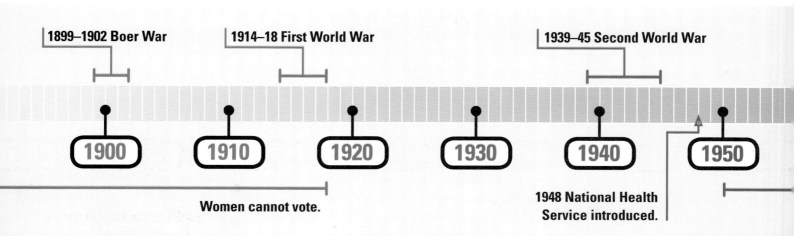

1899–1902 Boer War

1914–18 First World War

1939–45 Second World War

1900 1910 1920 1930 1940 1950

Women cannot vote.

1948 National Health Service introduced.

What is the significance of this event?

Significance

When you ask about the significance of something, you are thinking about what things it made happen and how much it changed things. This Live Aid concert raised over £150 million for people starving in Ethiopia. It also changed the way that people thought about charities and raising money for them.

Making a judgement

When you ask questions like the one below, you want to make a judgement. You will have evidence that suggests people did agree and evidence that people didn't. You can weigh up the balance of the evidence and decide what you think about it.

Did most people in Britain agree with the ideas in this poster in 1912?

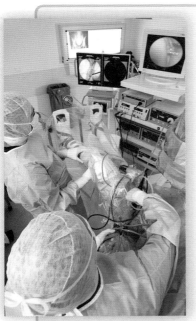

How much has medical practice changed since 1900?

Change and continuity

When you ask questions like the one above you are thinking about measuring change and continuity (ways in which things have and have not changed). You need to think about both of these things before you can really decide how much change has taken place.

What does this painting suggest about the impact of the First World War?

Impact

When you ask about the impact of an event you need to consider its effects and the ways in which it changed people's lives. For example, from the picture you can see that people died and friends and families were affected by this too. There was also lot of destruction which meant you couldn't grow things on this land or build on it.

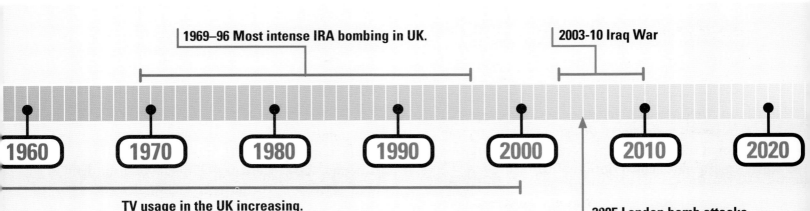

1969–96 Most intense IRA bombing in UK.

2003-10 Iraq War

| 1960 | 1970 | 1980 | 1990 | 2000 | 2010 | 2020 |

TV usage in the UK increasing.

2005 London bomb attacks

Causation

1.1 Why the rush to join up in 1914?

Lesson objectives

By the end of this lesson, you should be able to:
- explain why men rushed to **join up** in 1914
- understand that there were many reasons why men joined up
- understand that causes interact.

When historians talk about 'causation', they are talking about why things happened. There is very seldom just one cause for any event. When you think about why people do something the number of causes and how they affect each other are rarely the same for each person. Historians sometimes talk about 'causal webs' when they talking about causation. These look rather like spiders' webs with all the causes joined by lines to show how they affect each other. You are going to study causation by looking at why so many men in Britain joined the army when Britain went to war with Germany in 1914 at the start of the First World War.

Joining up in 1914

The First World War had been brewing for years. It involved many different countries, for different reasons. On both sides, young men responded to the call to join the army in huge numbers. Photographs show smiling, waving volunteers going to join up.

In August 1914, Britain had about 250,000 soldiers – about half of whom were serving abroad. Germany had about 700,000 soldiers. Lord Kitchener, the Minister for War, began a campaign to get men between 19 and 30 years of age to join up. The campaign used posters, advertisements in newspapers, and recruiting stations up and down the country. The government did not need to introduce **conscription** until 1916.

Kitchener hoped to get about 100,000 volunteers, but men volunteered at a rate of about 30,000 a day throughout August. Many were rejected as being too old, too young or not fit enough. Even so, many recruiting stations had to send hundreds of people away at the end of each day. Some rejected volunteers went from one recruiting station to another, hoping to find one that would take them.

By mid-September Kitchener had 500,000 men – far more than the army could train or equip all at once. Some had to wait months for training. Why were so many men so keen to join up, when they would be going away to face the dangers of war?

Source A: George Coppard was sixteen and a half when he joined up on 27 August 1914. He wrote about the war in his book, *With a Machine Gun to Cambrai*, in 1969.

News placards screamed out at every street corner and military bands blared out their military music in the main streets of Croydon. This was too much for me to resist and, as if drawn by a magnet, I knew I had to enlist straight away.

Source B: A young man from Canterbury, who joined the army as soon as Kitchener appealed, was interviewed about it later, in 1997.

Everyone was rushing to join – to join Kitchener's army, to have the honour of being one of the first hundred thousand.

Why did so many men in Britain rush to join up in 1914?

People joined up for many different reasons, or combinations of them. The most usual are shown on the next page. The image is the first recruitment poster of the war. The face is Lord Kitchener's.

Fighting for a 'just' cause

Many people felt Germany was in the wrong and had to be stopped. This feeling increased when Germany not only invaded **neutral** Belgium, but also treated civilians brutally. For example, the German army burned and looted the town of Louvain, shooting many people, including women and children, after it had surrendered.

Patriotism

The idea of 'serving your country' was central to the recruiting drive; at first, it was almost the only thing emphasised.

Ignorance

Very few of those who rushed to join up had any idea what fighting a war would be like. The general feeling was that Germany would be easily defeated; that the war would be over 'by Christmas'. Many men not taken as volunteers in the first few months were certain they had 'missed out' because of this belief.

BRITONS

"WANTS **YOU**"

JOIN YOUR COUNTRY'S ARMY!
GOD SAVE THE KING

Reproduced by permission of LONDON OPINION

Source C: A recruiting poster from the start of the war.

Influence of government propaganda

By 1915 the recruiting drive had changed emphasis from 'serving your country' to 'you're letting people down not joining up'. The idea of the brave soldier 'doing his bit' while others did nothing – leaving them in greater danger – was pushed home in various ways.

Public pressure

There was huge public pressure on young men to join up. People in the street asked them why they hadn't done so. The press urged men to join up and women to persuade them to do so. Some young women put notices like this in local newspapers: *If you aren't in uniform in two weeks time, I'll never speak to you again*. In September 1914, a group of 30 women in Kent gave white feathers (symbols of cowardice) to young men who weren't in uniform. The movement was soon at work country-wide.

Did you know?

Going too far?

Women of the White Feather Movement often gave feathers to the wrong people: soldiers on leave out of uniform; men who had fought but were unfit to go back; people in government jobs who could not join up. The government debated making giving out white feathers a crime, but settled for armbands and badges to show a person had a good reason not to be in the army.

Glossary

conscription: making people join the army

join up: join the military services of a country

a just cause: a reason for doing something that is morally right

neutral: a neutral country is one that has stated it will not get involved in the wars of other countries, on any side

Helping hand

When you are thinking about causes, don't forget that there is rarely one single cause for anything. This is why historians often talk about 'causation webs' – linked causes that feed each other.

Activity

A young man, Stan, who had not joined up in 1914 leaves home to go to work. By the time he returns home, he has joined up. You are going to draw a causal web of all the reasons why Stan did this.

1. First, read about Stan's day. As you do so, list the reasons that build up during the day. The first one would be guilt because he feels bad about the neighbour's son.

Source D: A recruiting poster from 1915.

Stan's Day

As he walks to the station Stan sees a neighbour whose son has just been killed in the war. The neighbour used to be friendly, now she ignores him. Outside the train station a young woman he knows smiles at him. He walks over to talk to her. She hands him a white feather and walks off, not speaking. The station is full of posters urging men to join up.

The paper Stan reads on the train talks about the urgent need for more volunteers. At work, one man talks about his son, away fighting, with huge pride. Another says he can't persuade his son to join up. Other listeners shake their heads sadly. Someone asks Stan why he hasn't joined up yet. There is a long silence. Stan struggles to find an answer.

On the way home, Stan passes a recruiting station. A recruiting sergeant calls out to him. Stan pauses. The recruiting sergeant walks over and talks to Stan about joining up. The sergeant talks about Stan's country needing him and 'the lads out there' needing him. He talks about 'doing the right thing'. Stan joins up.

When he gets home Stan tells his parents he has joined up. They ask why. He says the recruiting sergeant made him feel it was time to serve his country. He gives one reason, but it was probably the build-up of causes through the day. He might not have joined up on that day if the sergeant hadn't talked to him, but this wasn't the only cause.

Activity

2. Draw a circle in the middle of a piece of paper and write in it Stan joins up.

3. List the reasons and put them into separate boxes on the paper, each with an arrow leading to the centre box. Use a word or a short phrase each time (for example, neighbour ignores him).

4. Now join causes that you think are linked (for example, all those that are to do with Stan feeling guilty), using lines with an arrow at each end.

Conscientious objectors

While tens of thousands of men rushed to join up in 1914 and 1915, some men refused to do so, for reasons of conscience. They called themselves 'conscientious objectors' – they objected to fighting a war. They did this for various reasons.

- **Religious reasons**
  Some people were conscientious objectors for religious reasons, for example people who were Quakers. They believed that God said it was wrong to go to war and it was more important to them that they obey God rather than the government.

- **Moral reasons**
  Some people believed that war was wrong because they believed that you should not kill another person. They did not necessarily follow any particular religion, but they did have beliefs about what was right and wrong that affected how they acted.

- **Reasons to do with the First World War**
  Some people did not object to the idea of war, but they did object to war with Germany. Usually these people had family or business connections with Germany.

- **Political reasons**
  Some political groups, such as the Socialists, believed their political movement was a world-wide one. Because of this, they felt that British Socialists should not fight German Socialists, which would happen if they had to join the army.

- **Fear**
  There were some people who did not want to go to war. They said they were conscientious objectors because it gave them a reason for not joining up.

Some conscientious objectors were willing to go to war, but not to fight. Over 3,000 of them drove ambulances or carried stretchers on battlefields, justifying their war work because what they did stopped people suffering. Many conscientious objectors refused to do this, because they said any war work (no matter if it saved lives) was working under military orders, so was still wrong.

When conscription was introduced, in January 1916, people had to register as conscientious objectors and go to a hearing to explain to officials – including people from the army – why they did not want to fight. If the officials at the hearing believed they were really conscientious objectors, they were given an exemption certificate.

Exemption certificates meant conscientious objectors did not have to fight, but they were expected to do war-work such as working in hospitals. If they refused to do so they were imprisoned or sent to labour camps, working in mines or quarries.

Activity

5. a) Read the headings of the causes for joining up that are around the poster on page 9. Look at your causal web for Stan.

   b) Are there any of those causes that are not represented on Stan's web? Write a short paragraph to explain what it/they are, and whether you think they would have affected Stan or not.

   c) Write a paragraph to explain which of these reasons that applied to men joining up, might also apply to the women who pressured men to join up.

6. Make a causal web like the one you made for Stan, on the reasons for becoming a conscientious objector.

Making a judgement

In this lesson, you have seen that young men joined up for a complex set of reasons. Public pressure was often a big factor. People called conscientious objectors were often labelled as cowards for not going to fight. Think about what they might say in reply, about their reasons for not joining up and whether resisting such pressure was 'cowardly', especially after the introduction of conscription.

Consequence

1.2 What effect did the First World War have on the Votes for Women campaign?

Lesson objectives

By the end of this lesson, you should be able to:

- understand attitudes to the **suffragette cause** before and after the First World War
- describe how attitudes to women were affected by their war work
- explain the consequences of the First World War for the Votes for Women campaign.

Historians often need to consider the effects, or consequences, of an event. Events usually have more than one consequence. You are going to study consequence by looking at changing attitudes to the campaign to get women the vote.

In the 19th century, voting was restricted to a small number of men, but women had campaigned for the right to vote (suffrage) since the 1860s. They gave out leaflets, held public meetings and wrote to MPs explaining their views. In 1897 the National Union of Women's Suffrage Societies (NUWSS) was set up to campaign for the vote.

Why not give women the vote?

Many people were against giving women the vote – men and women of all ages. They had various reasons for this, the most often ones given were:

Women are too emotional. They can't think clearly enough to vote responsibly

Women and men have different roles. A woman's place is in the home. Men take care of business and politics.

Source A: An anti-sufragette cartoon showing the fear that women would neglect their homes and families.

Well I'm ____

Women aren't clever enough to vote. They will vote for the handsome candidate.

Women don't fight in wars or run businesses. They shouldn't take part in government.

Activity

1. If women were given the vote, what did the opponents of Votes for Women think the effects might be on:

   a) homes and families

   b) the kinds of people who would be elected?

The WSPU

In 1903 the Women's Social and Political Union (WSPU) was set up with the motto 'Deeds not Words'. They campaigned more actively than the NUWSS, even breaking the law to gain publicity. They interrupted parliamentary debates and chained themselves to railings. They chose to go to prison rather than pay fines when they broke the law, getting the nickname 'suffragettes' for their more militant activities. The results of all this were:

- they gained even more publicity

- they provoked debate and growing support

- they did not get the vote.

Because they still had no vote, some suffragettes became more violent. They began by smashing the windows of shopfronts and politicians' houses. By 1914 some were destroying property (including setting letterboxes on fire to destroy the letters inside), setting fire to MPs' homes and attacking police.

One effect of this growing violence was that the campaign for the vote lost support; other suffrage groups criticised the WSPU. Another effect was that opponents said women who broke the law and damaged property did not deserve the vote. They also pointed to the disagreement between suffragettes and suffragists, saying that if women couldn't work together for the same aim, they should not have the vote.

Glossary

cause: something you believe in and want to make happen

suffragette: the nickname given to members of the WSPU who were prepared to use extreme methods to get the vote for women

suffragist: someone who believed in peaceful methods of campaigning for the vote for women

1897: National Union of Women's Suffrage Societies set up

1908: First window smashing. Number of arrests rise rapidly. Membership of WSPU rises too

1913: Firebombs, post boxes set alight. Public and police violence against suffragettes grows

1903: Women's Social and Political Union (WSPU) set up

1909: First hunger strikes of suffragette prisoners. They are forcibly fed

1906: First suffragette arrests, at House of Commons

1912: Violence more common. Support drops

1911: Law gives the vote to more men; no women. Widespread window smashing, vandalism and arrests

1914: Britain goes to war. Suffragettes campaign for women to be allowed to help by working

1913: MPs homes targeted. Emily Davison throws herself under horses at Derby Day races

1910: Government consider giving votes to women. Suffragettes campaign peacefully. Much support

Activity

2. a) Use the information above to make a timeline for the campaign for votes for women up to the outbreak of war.

   b) Put a smiley emoticon at the point where you think the suffragettes had most support and a sad emoticon where you feel they had least support.

   c) Give one effect of the increased WSPU violence from 1911.

14

War

By 1914, the WSPU was widely seen as having damaged the campaign for the vote. Then the First World War broke out. The WSPU stopped its violent action at once. It began campaigning instead for the right of women to help the war effort. At first, the government wasn't sure that women could, or should, do war work. But in the end they asked women to help – they needed women workers, with so many men going off to fight.

At first, there were many places where women were not made welcome by the men still working there and who had the job of training them. Some had a hard time gaining acceptance, because the men felt they would be a burden, not a help. But, as the war progressed, so many women proved to be useful that they gained acceptance.

Working women

By the end of the war over two million women had taken over the jobs of men who had gone to fight. They worked in government offices, factories, mines, on public transport, in the police and on farms. They took over family businesses – from sweeping chimneys and running shops, to running funeral homes and digging graves. Thousands more worked in the armed services as nurses, drivers, canteen workers and clerks.

Not all women who worked during the war wanted the vote, they just wanted to help. But they showed what women could do. Of course, not all women worked and not all women managed well, but the fact that a large number of them did, resulted in people thinking differently about how responsible and capable most women were.

Consequences of war work

The work that women did in the war showed people that many of their assumptions about women were wrong. It had been assumed by many that women:

- **could not do the same work as men:** women actually did heavy work, such as mining.

- **could not make clear-headed decisions:** many women had to run family businesses, organise canteens or drive ambulances to and from battlefields.

- **were not as intelligent as men:** women showed they could think and plan as efficiently. The fact that many women managed to live independently – running the family and working, while so many men were away at the front – was a surprise to some people.

In 1917 Herbert Asquith, the ex-Prime Minister who had been a fierce opponent of votes for women, said that at least some women should be given the vote. He said this was as a consequence of their war work, and also the fact that suffragettes had stopped using violence. 'How could we have carried on the war without women?' he asked.

With such a well-known opponent changing his mind, others followed. However, the war work that women had done did not have the same effect on everyone. Some people still firmly believed that no women should be allowed to vote. They saw voting as a different issue.

Helping hand

When talking about the consequences of something it is important to clearly link the consequence back to the event or action. Use phrases such as, *'one consequence of this'*, *'as a result'*, *'because of this'*. Be careful to explain the connection between the event or action and the consequence described – say how the action produced the consequence.

Don't say, *'there was more support for Votes for Women after the war because women had worked during it'*.

Do say, *'there was more support for Votes for Women after the war because women had worked during it and had shown they were more capable than many people had thought, and were loyal to their country'*.

Activity

3. Think about the three examples on this page of ways in which women's war work showed that some assumptions about women were wrong. Write a sentence for each assumption, choosing one type of war work and saying how it would affect the assumption.

Campaigning after the war

When the war ended, women pressed for the vote again. This time, the suffragettes did not turn to violence. This was because they remembered how public opinion had shifted away from supporting them when they had campaigned violently. They also realised that politicians were coming round to the idea of votes for women, which had a lot of public support. If they campaigned violently it would make it harder for politicians to support their campaign.

The 1918 Act

In 1918 The Representation of the People Act was passed. It gave more men the vote. It also gave women over 30 who owned or rented property (or were married to someone who did) the vote. Women were also allowed to stand as MPs. In the 1918 elections, 40 per cent of all those who voted were women. In the election of 1919 Nancy Astor became the first woman MP to take her seat in the House of Commons.

Source B: A mother voting in the December 1918 elections.

Activity

4. Write a paragraph explaining how people felt about votes for women in 1918. Explain what might have affected their feelings.

5. Copy out the sentence below that you feel is the most accurate. Write a sentence to explain your choice.
   - One of the consequences of the First World War was that women in Britain got the vote.
   - One of the consequences of women working during the First World War was that people saw them as responsible enough to have the vote.
   - One of the consequences of the work that women did during the First World War was that more politicians voted for women to get the vote.
   - One of the consequences of the work that women did during the First World War was that women in Britain got the vote.

6. Copy and complete the following sentence. Votes for women became more likely when the WSPU changed their tactics after the war began and...

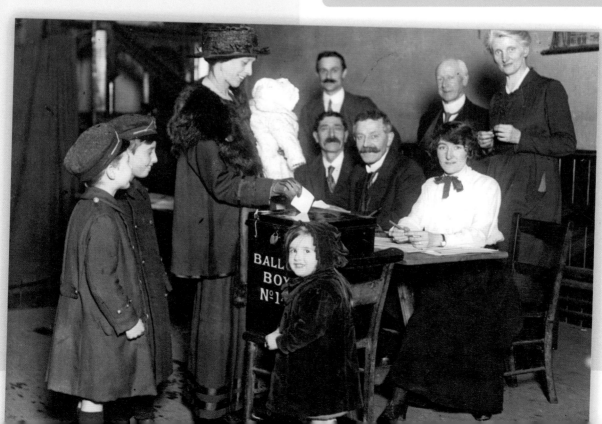

Making a judgement

1.3 Home Front propaganda in the Second World War

Lesson objectives

By the end of this lesson, you should be able to:
- discuss how the MOI used **propaganda** during the Second World War
- explain the process of making a judgement
- make a judgement on a question.

This lesson focuses on making a judgement. You will consider a question and reach your own judgement on it, from the evidence in these pages. You will be considering government propaganda in the Second World War.

On 3 September 1939, Britain and France declared war on Germany. The war had been building up for years and the government had been preparing for it. One new department it set up during the war was the Ministry of Information (MOI). Its job was to stop information getting out that might help the enemy. It also spread government propaganda. MOI propaganda was everywhere during the war. One of the things it wanted to do was to change the way that people in Britain behaved, to help the government. Did it work? Did people change the way they behaved? That's the judgement you will be making using the evidence provided.

What kind of propaganda?

During the war the MOI asked people to: grow their own food, use less coal, use less petrol, eat less bread, buy less, mend their own clothes and re-use fabric, use the telephone less, do war work and be careful what they talked about in public. It was, in fact, a pretty constant stream of demands. It also explained things, including how to put on gas masks, what to do in an air raid, how to grow your own food and how to behave in the **blackout**.

MOI propaganda came as:
- posters
- newspaper inserts
- radio announcements and programmes. The MOI advised but didn't control BBC broadcasts
- films: information films; short 'news' films and feature films with a patriotic message
- information pamphlets explaining how to do things (keep rabbits to eat, grow vegetables).

Effective propaganda

Propaganda could be seen as effective if people started behaving in the 'right' way. For MOI propaganda to be effective it had to:
- express itself well
- be memorable
- reach a wide range of people
- convince people.

The MOI's first campaign used a poster that said: *Your Courage, Your Cheerfulness, Your Resolution will Bring us Victory*. A survey showed that people thought the 'your' and 'us' separated the people from the government and that the slogan wasn't short enough or memorable enough.

Did it work?

Reactions to MOI campaigns varied. Campaigns that gave people a sense of helping the war effort were usually effective.

Did you know?

MOI slogan writing improved with time. *Don't Help the Enemy, Careless Talk May Give Away Vital Secrets* was accurate, but the later version, *Careless Talk Costs Lives*, was a far better slogan.

The campaigns to collect food scraps for pigs and scrap metal for planes both got a huge response; boy scouts arranged collections and groups competed with each other to collect the most.

The *Careless Talk Costs Lives* campaign also made a big impression on most people. It was so effective that some people even interrupted conversations between strangers on the bus to tell them off if they thought they were talking about things that should not be discussed in public, such as where **munitions** factories were.

On the other hand, the *Is Your Journey Really Necessary?* campaign to get people to travel less, so that more trains could carry munitions, was not very effective. Someone pointed out that whenever not travelling was inconvenient people would say 'Yes, my journey is necessary'.

Some MOI propaganda backfired badly. A poster urging mothers whose children were **evacuees** to leave them safe in the country not bring them home, just reminded mothers that they missed their children. The campaign may even have increased the number of returning evacuees.

Other factors?

When considering how effective propaganda is you also need to consider other factors that might push people in the same direction as the propaganda. For example, the pressure to 'grow your own' was helped by both food **rationing** and food shortages – it made sense to people to grow as much as they could. The campaign to get people to travel less was helped by the overcrowding and long delays that became usual on passenger trains, as well as by the withdrawal of cheap day return tickets.

Activity

1. List the following campaigns under the headings 'Effective', 'Not effective' and 'Helped by other factors':

   travel less; grow your own food; collect pig food; collect scrap metal; don't gossip in public; leave evacuees in the countryside.

Source A: An MOI poster encouraging people to grow their own food so ships coming to Britain could carry war supplies not food. The poster was first used in 1942.

USE SPADES NOT SHIPS

GROW YOUR OWN FOOD

AND SUPPLY YOUR OWN COOKHOUSE

Glossary

blackout: stopping any lights showing after dark, so enemy bombers couldn't tell where the towns and cities were

evacuees: children sent out of the cities (which the government feared would be bombed) to the countryside

munitions: weapons of various sorts

propaganda: public information given to people to affect the way they think and behave

rationing: restricting how much of certain foods or other goods each person can buy

18

Source B: From the diary of Christopher Tomlin, a young man in his late twenties living in London.

5 January 1940: It's a good job I am not spying for the enemy. A young couple on the bus in front of me chatted about the movement of troops from Preston. The girl said when the local searchlight battalion were off to Scapa Flow and when the North Lancs were off to France. She mentioned six lots of troops in all. What a little fool!

Source C: One of the many *Careless Talk Costs Lives* cartoon posters by the cartoonist Fougasse. Hitler and Air Vice Marshall Goering are riding in the seats behind the gossiping women.

Source D: From the diary of 38 year old Pam Ashford, a secretary in a coal shipping firm in Glasgow.

4 March 1941: I heard today that the King and Queen will be visiting the Glasgow shipyards tomorrow.
5 March 1940: Charlie [her brother] left for work [in the shipyards] early. Mother asked if he was going to meet the King and Queen. Before going to work, I impressed on mother the need to keep her lips tight shut. "You don't want the King and Queen bumped off because of an indiscreet word of yours!"

Source E: From an interview with Ivy Gross, a 28 year old insurance agent.

'All my customers listened to the radio a lot and I'd have a cup of tea with some of them and we'd talk about listening to Churchill's latest speech, or the recipes from the Ministry of Food. Most of us believed the news; you trusted the BBC to tell you what was going on, though not all of what was going on. We talked about the MOI posters we liked the best – there was a bit of competition about who would spot the latest Fougasse *Careless Talk* one.

Activity

Use all the sources on this page and the information on the previous page.

2. Think about Source C as a piece of government propaganda. Was it successful? Write a sentence to explain how far you think it met each of the following:

   a) it expresses itself well

   b) it is memorable

   c) it reached a wide range of people

   d) it convinced people.

3. Look at Source A. Write a paragraph explaining how the artist has managed to get across the message of the slogan.

A lasting effect?

One way of judging if the MOI's propaganda was effective is to see if there is evidence that people changed the way they behaved. Another way of measuring effectiveness is how much the new behaviour became built into people's lives.

After the war was over and rationing stopped Britain began to get back to 'normal'. People went back to their old travelling ways as soon as they could. However, not all war-time behaviour was abandoned as quickly. Many people kept on growing their own food, although people who had dug up their whole garden often only kept part of it as a vegetable garden. But 'doing the garden' had become a habit – one that many people would not have had if they had not been pushed into it by necessity during the war.

Helping hand

When you are making a judgement about something you are usually trying to work out how important that something is or was, how far you agree with a statement, or if one single cause was the main reason for an event.

In all these cases, you must outline the evidence for *and* against, then give your judgement. The judgement you reach is less important than showing how you have reached it. You need to show that you have considered all the evidence, giving detail from the evidence to back up your thinking.

Did you know?

The Dig for Victory campaign was a huge success. Over a million new allotments were started and people dug up their own gardens. Almost everyone who could, grew their own vegetables. If they had no gardens they rented an allotment, or dug the garden of an elderly neighbour, sharing the vegetables. Vegetables were grown in the most unlikely places – including the moat of the Tower of London! More and more people kept chickens, rabbits and goats, especially when eggs, milk and meat were rationed and hard to get.

Activity

You are going to plan an answer to the question

'*How effective was Ministry of Information propaganda in getting people to do what the government wanted during the Second World War?*'

The following questions will take you through the planning, step by step.

4. Read the question carefully. You will need to make it clear in your answer:
   - that you understand what propaganda is
   - that you have an idea about what makes propaganda successful
   - that you have considered the effectiveness of MOI propaganda in the Second World War.

5. Write a sentence defining propaganda.

6. Write a short paragraph saying what you think makes propaganda successful.

Your answers to Activities 5 and 6 would form the start of your answer.

7. Use the three lists you made for the Activity on page 17. Add some detail to each campaign that explains why you have put it in a particular list.

   If you were writing an essay, you would make each list into a paragraph, using phrases like *on the one hand there is evidence to suggest, on the other hand, other evidence suggests*. These paragraphs are particularly important, as they explain what you are basing your judgement on.

8. Write a summing up paragraph – your judgement – using the following framework:
   The information I have been given suggests to me ....

   I think this because on the one hand, ...

   On the other hand, ...

   So, overall, ...

Significance

1.4 The National Health Service

Lesson objectives

By the end of this lesson, you should be able to:
- explain how the NHS was set up and worked
- understand how to evaluate the significance of a person or event.

When historians evaluate the significance of people or events they are asking the question "what difference did they make?" They are asking how an event or person brought about change or affected people's lives in other ways. To do this, you need to understand the situation before and after. You also need to understand that, while someone or something has to affect a large number of people to be seen as significant, it will have different types of effect on different people. You will be thinking about this in relation to the setting up of the National Health Service (NHS), which is seen as an important post-war event.

On 5 July 1948, the NHS was launched to provide free healthcare for everyone in Britain.

The situation before 1948

In 1900 most people had to pay for their own healthcare. There was no national healthcare system. Some employers and some trade unions ran insurance schemes where a worker could choose to pay into the scheme then get some money back if they were too ill to work.

In 1911 the government set up National Health Insurance for workers in some industries (such as shipbuilding). The government, the employers and the workers all had to pay into a fund that provided some healthcare and sick pay for the workers in the relevant industries. This helped some of the workers, but there was no healthcare for their families, and workers in industries that were not part of the National Health Insurance scheme still had no healthcare.

How the NHS began

The government set up the NHS by **nationalising** the healthcare that was already available. This meant all opticians, dentists and GPs, who had been working for themselves, now worked for the government. The government, not the patient, paid their fees.

Private hospitals and those run by local government under the National Insurance Scheme were now run by the NHS. Because it did not have to build new hospitals or clinics immediately, the NHS could start running straight away in July 1948. However, this caused a problem. Many more people went to the doctor, dentist, optician or hospital, now that they did not have to pay for healthcare. This meant the number of patients rose, while the number of places to care for them did not.

Public reaction

The public was in favour of the NHS, but there was a struggle to get doctors and other healthcare professionals to accept it. The doctors did not like the idea of having to work for the government, instead of working for themselves anymore.

The introduction of the NHS was a huge change, and a huge benefit. Anyone in the country could get free healthcare anywhere in the country (it did not matter if you were away from home in a different part of the country when you needed treatment). So as soon as the NHS was launched, there was an overwhelming demand for almost all the services. People who had been living with various health problems because they could not afford treatment, rushed to get it. In December 1948 the Minister of Health, Aneurin Bevan, had to tell MPs that the estimated cost of £176 million for the NHS in 1948–49 would actually be nearer to £225 million!

Opticians

Opticians charged for consultation and any treatment, including glasses.

Not that many people went to see an optician. Many people with more minor eyesight problems did not even realise they had them.

Dentists

Dentists charged for both check-up and treatment.

The only dentistry many poor people ever had was when they had painful teeth pulled out by a barber. Even better-off people often only went to the dentist if their teeth hurt or broke.

Medicine

Medicine and treatment all had to be paid for.

Some poor people made the difficult decision to call in (and pay) a doctor only to find they could not pay for the treatment he prescribed.

What was healthcare like before the NHS?

Hospitals

Most hospitals charged a fee.

There was some free treatment, but it depended on where you lived. Some free hospitals were set up by charities or other organisations. These were either very simple general hospitals or hospitals treating one type of disease. Some hospitals did treat accident victims for free.

Doctors

Most doctors charged a fee.

Some doctors treated patients free under the National Health Insurance scheme or in clinics set up by various organisations. Some chose to treat poor people for free, or at a lower cost.

The poor were less able to afford treatment, and this treatment was often given in less healthy conditions than private treatment.

Activity

1. Look at the diagram of healthcare before the NHS. Write a short paragraph to explain how the creation of the NHS might have affected the following people in 1948:

   a) a rich middle-aged woman with asthma who lived in London

   b) the pregnant wife of a fisherman in Cornwall, who already had three children

   c) a shipbuilder in Newcastle-upon-Tyne who needed an operation.

Glossary

mortality rate: the number of people in certain categories (e.g., age groups, region they live in) who die

nationalise: when the state takes over the running of an industry

The NHS settles down

The high levels of demand for NHS treatment led to some panic among MPs about its cost. The 1948-49 costs actually came to just under £280 million. The following year costs were £449 million. By this point, the government had voted to put a charge on prescriptions, and to charge for dental and eye care. These charges did not apply, however, to the elderly, to people earning below a certain income, or to those with a disability. So healthcare was still available and affordable to all.

By 1951, things had settled down. The first rush for treatment had slowed. Costs had levelled off. Government and newspaper debate had made many people aware that unnecessary use of services was damaging the system, that there wasn't unlimited funding for everyone. Despite their protests against the setting up of the NHS, over 95 per cent of all doctors had joined it by 1950.

Source B: From the National Archives website article on the NHS, written in the 1990s.

Between 1948 and 1973 the number of doctors doubled. Anaesthetics continued to advance, enabling longer and more complex surgery. The NHS improved the lives of millions with hip replacement operations, emergency treatment for accident victims, and fertility treatment for childless couples. Programmes of vaccination protected children from whooping cough, measles, tuberculosis and diphtheria. New technology enabled brain and whole body scans, and advances were made in the care of the mentally ill. Even cosmetic surgery became available on the NHS.

Helping hand

When you are considering the significance of a person or event, remember that the effect these have will vary from person to person. So the setting up of the NHS, for example, had a huge effect on the lives of some people, but made little difference to people in different circumstances. Make sure you are clear in your answer that you understand this, giving specific examples to show the different effects (as you are asked to do in the Activity on page 21).

Source A: A midwife on a home visit in 1965. The care provided by clinics, hospitals and midwives before, during and after birth meant that from 1948 there were far fewer deaths of babies and mothers.

Longer term effects

Over a longer span of time it became apparent that the NHS was having a positive effect on the nation's health:

- Its vaccination programmes were drastically cutting the **mortality rate** from childhood diseases such as whooping cough, diphtheria and measles. For example, in 1940 there were 409,521 cases of measles, of which 850 were fatal. In 1981 there were 97,408 cases and only 11 deaths.

- Older people were living longer.

- Many people who might have died resulting from a wide range of accidents were getting treatment quickly and therefore surviving.

- New equipment, such as MRI scanners, helped doctors to diagnose diseases sooner.

Source C: Deaths of babies under a year old, showing the number of deaths per 1000 born alive.

Years	Deaths per 1000
1936 – 40	55
1941 – 45	50
1946 – 50	36
1951 – 55	27
1956 – 60	23
1961 – 65	21
1966 – 70	18
1971 – 75	17
1976 – 80	13

Source D: Approximate number of hospital doctors and nurses for every 10,000 people in England and Wales.

Year	Nurses	Doctors
1931	38	7
1941	42	7
1951	47	8
1961	58	10
1971	62	11
1981	69	12

Activity

2. List at least three ways in which the NHS was able to improve the health of babies and young children. Give detail to support each example.

3. In 1949, how might the NHS have had a significant effect on:

   a) how long a poor person waited before going to the doctor with stomach pains

   b) how effective the treatment was for the problem they had?

4. Do you think your answer would be any different for 1989? Write a sentence to explain what you think and why.

5. Write two sentences explaining what the significance of the newly created NHS was.

Helping hand

When you are deciding about the significance of a person or event, remember that other factors will have made an impact. Try to provide examples of other possible factors that could have had an impact to show that you understand this.

For example, while the care provided by the NHS undoubtedly had effect on infant mortality, it is unlikely that it was the only factor responsible for the drop in infant mortality shown in Source C. Improved living conditions probably also played a part, for example. If you cannot think of an example, you should at least make the general point that other factors will have played a part'.

Making a judgement

In this lesson, you have considered the significance of the setting up of the NHS and the free healthcare it provided. Do you think the later introduction of charges made it less significant?

Change

1.5 How getting the news has changed

24

Lesson objectives

By the end of this lesson, you should be able to:
- understand how reporting the news has changed
- understand why these changes have come about
- consider the extent of change
- weigh up the significance of these changes.

In the course of the 20th century, Britain went to war many times. We are going to look at changes in how the **media** brought news of three of these wars to Britain over the years. We will be thinking about what form the news came in (media), who had access to it and how quickly it arrived.

The Boer War: 1899–1902

In 1900, the British were at war in South Africa. They were fighting the Boers – the descendants of the original Dutch settlers there. There were battles and several towns were besieged, including Ladysmith, where the siege was broken in 1900.

People in Britain got news of the war mainly in newspapers and magazines. This was the first war since primary education had been made compulsory in 1870. Many more people could read than ever before and the number of newspapers and magazines had grown rapidly to meet the new demand. While *The Times* cost **3d**, the new *Daily Mail* only cost 1d. But in 1900 many poorer families, even with family members working, were not earning enough to cover their basic needs, let alone buy a newspaper.

News was usually printed a day or two after the event. It was sent by telegraph. Photographs and sketches (used in magazines) had to be sent by post, so took over a week to arrive.

Newspapers and magazines were not the only way new of the war reached the British public. Four different companies sent people to record the war on film. William Kennedy-Laurie Dickson, of the Biograph Company was one of them. Film was a new technology and the equipment was heavy and took a long time to set up. This meant that the film-makers could not film battles. They filmed troops on the march, army camps and action from a distance. There was no commentary to go with the films.

Source A: From a book by William Dickson about filming the Boer War. It was printed in 1901.

Getting back to a safer position, we watched the valiant attack of our men as they gradually pushed on. Had we a light camera these movements could have been filmed, and many others of a valuable nature, but the enormous bulk of our apparatus which had to be dragged about in a cart with two horses, prevented our getting to the spot. The difficulties were worsened by the absence of roads, the huge gullies we had to cross and the enormous boulders we had to get over.

Source B: An artist's impression of troops at Mafeking in 1900.

The Second World War: 1939–45

The Second World War was fought by many nations, in many different parts of the world. Some nations only fought for part of the duration of the war. Britain was one of the nations that fought the whole time, in many different parts of the world. During the war, news of the fighting in other countries still reached people in Britain by newspaper, as it had during the Boer War.

Newsreels were shown in every cinema, all over the country. Filming equipment had improved since the Boer War. It was lighter, quicker to use and giving a better quality of film. There were now spoken commentaries with the newsreels, telling people what was happening. Films were usually in cinemas within a week of the event they showed.

The biggest change was that now almost every home had a radio, or neighbours with a radio. The radio was vital in bringing news as well as entertainment. News often reached Britain the same day, or within a day or two of events. Much of the news was summaries of what was going on, but there were some broadcasts of events as they occurred.

Source C: The opening screen of a newsreel report on British troops advancing in Italy in 1943.

Helping hand

When you write about how things have changed it is important that you give specific examples wherever possible. It is also important that you think about, and describe, things that have stayed the same.

So don't say, *In 1940 there were more ways than just newspapers and film of getting the news than in 1900.*

Do say, *In 1940 newspapers were still an important way to find out about the news but there were changes. Films now had a commentary to tell you what was going on in the film. Radio was a new, and very important, way of getting the news that was widely available.*

Source D: From the diary of Clara Milburn, an Englishwoman who lived in a village near Coventry. She wrote this on 23 January 1943.

Good news! Tripoli is in our hands. Fourteen hundred miles the Eighth Army has advanced in 80 days, over desert sand and scrub, tank-traps, mines and booby-traps, but nothing stopped them. They went on advancing.

Glossary

3d: three pennies in pre-decimal currency (the same price as a loaf of bread)

media: ways of mass communication

coalition: an alliance of different countries that is not permanent, but made for one particular action

anonymously: acting without giving your name

2003–10: The Iraq War

In 2003 Britain was at war in Iraq. By now, advances in technology meant that there were many new ways of getting the news and the old ways were able to report the news much more quickly. The intensive bombing of Iraq by **coalition** forces, mainly from the USA and Britain, began on 19 March 2003.

The attack on Baghdad on 21 March 2003 was reported live on TV and radio world-wide. It was reported in the newspapers the next day. Advances in computer technology meant that people could also get the news online – from official newspaper and broadcasting websites.

Most people in Britain had access to one or other of the many ways of getting the news at this point – newspapers, radio, TV and computers. They may not have used it, for a variety of reasons, but in 2003 the news was far more accessible than ever before.

> **Source E**: *The Times* report of the bombing of Baghdad on the 21 March 2003.

Reacting to news, creating news

During the Iraq War, people could respond publicly to the news as it happened. They could go online and discuss the war, rather than just talk about it with friends, colleagues and family. Online blogs and debates gave people a new way to feel involved in the news, and many of them used it to protest at Britain's involvement in the war.

The website *Wikileaks* (which first went online in 2006) created a new news format. People could post information on the site **anonymously**. This meant they could post without fear of harm coming to them as a result. Thousands of documents, mostly concerning the actions of governments world-wide, have been posted. *Wikileaks* insists that their posts are checked by several editors before they are posted, to assess whether they are actual documents or fakes. In 2010, the site posted secret US military logs, over 300,000 reports that showed how the US conducted the war. These documents were then broadcast by other media.

THE TIMES

No. 67717   SATURDAY MARCH 22 2003   4AM 5L 5L   www.timesonline.co.uk

The blitzing of Baghdad

From Roland Watson and Elaine Monaghan in Washington

BRITISH and American forces rained thunder on the heart of Baghdad last night in a blitzkrieg designed to terrify Iraqi leaders and their Republican Guard into surrender.

Wave upon wave of bombs and missiles triggered deafening explosions and giant fireballs that left buildings ablaze and sent towering plumes of red, pink and thick brown smoke into the sky.

The relentless onslaught of a thousand cruise missiles and a thousand airstrikes was precisely aimed at President Saddam Hussein's political and military power base. Fires raged at his palace complexes and key government buildings as tracer fire from anti-aircraft batteries arced overhead. Several hundred military targets around the country were also attacked.

The strategy appeared to pay immediate dividends when an entire division of some 8,000 men was reported to have surrendered to US Marines advancing towards Basra, Iraq's second city. The 51st Division, whose task was to protect the key oil shipment hub, was one of Iraq's better equipped forces, with about 200 tanks before the war.

The bombing of Iraq was intensified after American officials revealed that special forces had been negotiating with Republican Guard leaders. The awesome display of firepower was designed as much to increase the pressure on them to surrender as to destroy targets vital to Saddam.

Announcing the start of the air war, Donald Rumsfeld, the US Defence Secretary, said the goal was to strike "with force on a scope and scale that makes clear to Iraqis that he [Saddam] and his regime are finished. With the start of the air war it may be that we find people responding."

Surrender talks between coalition forces and Iraqi chiefs have gathered pace in recent days

Smoke from a cruise missile strike covers the presidential complex in Baghdad, seen from the left bank of the River Tigris, from the top of the Palestine Meridian Hotel. Photograph by Ramzi Haidar / AP

By the time of the Iraq War, news coverage had become a tactic in war. The reporter Allan Little has given many talks on reporting on the Iraq War. In a talk on 4 October 1010, at the University of Lincoln, he said that the news that reporters sent home was seen as part of the military campaign. It was too risky not to be 'embedded' – reporters had to move with the coalition forces rather than go out alone for a story. This gave the armed forces far more control over the news because the reporters were only allowed to go where they were told.

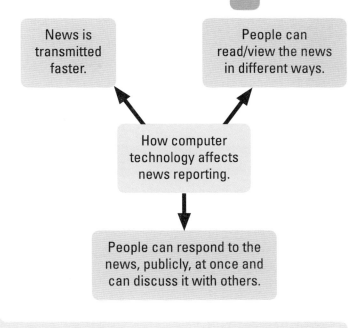

News is transmitted faster.

People can read/view the news in different ways.

How computer technology affects news reporting.

People can respond to the news, publicly, at once and can discuss it with others.

Activity

1. a) Give one way that ways of reporting the news changed between 1900 and 1940.
    b) Give one way that ways of reporting the news changed between 1940 and 2003.
    c) Give one way that ways of reporting the news remained the same between 1900 and 2003.

2. Read Source A. Think about how it shows the general problems faced by new technologies. Write a paragraph to describe this.

3. Draw a diagram like the one on the right and write 'Who has access to the news is affected by...' in the centre box. Complete the other boxes

4. Write a short paragraph for each of the following, explaining how they changed between 1900 and 2000 (refer to sources where useful):
    *   the speed at which we get the news
    *   the media that provides the news
    *   the number of people who have access to the news.

The technology reporters can use to send the news. (eg. modern satellite technology)

The access reporters have to the technology when reporting.

How fast we get the news is affected by ...

The access we have to media: newspapers, TV, radio and computer media

How easily and quickly the equipment, and reporters, can be moved

Making a judgement

In this lesson, you have seen how the invention of different means of communication has affected how people get the news each day. Which do you think is the most significant change in the way we get the news:

*   how soon we get the news
*   how many people have access to the news
*   the way we get the news?

Continuity

28

1.6 Targeting civilians

Lesson objectives

By the end of this lesson, you should be able to:

- explain the targeting of civilians in Britain during the 20th century
- understand the concept of continuity
- consider continuity over time.

When historians think about continuity (how things have stayed the same over time), they compare the situation over time, noting both the things that stay the same and those that change. In the course of the 20th century, in times of war and in peacetime, British civilians were the target of various groups. You are going to consider continuity within this context.

Wartime bombing: 1915–18

The first 20th century example of British civilians being used as targets was during the First World War. First, German airships, called zeppelins, then German planes, bombed London and other British cities from 1915 to 1918.

The German government wanted the British government to surrender. It felt that targeting civilians would make the general population fearful, stop them supporting the war and push for surrender instead. During about a hundred raids they killed 1,413 people and injured 3,409. German bombs destroyed hundreds of homes and shops as well as disrupting services such as water, electricity and gas.

Activity

1. As you read through the examples of the use of civilians as targets, make notes on:
- who is targeting the civilians and why
- how the targeting is done (weapons, scale – i.e. size, number etc.)
- the impact the targeting has (scale of devastation, areas of life affected, how many affected).

This will help you to think about the ways in which things are the same or how they differ.

Source A: A street in the East End of London after a zeppelin raid on 31 January 1916.

The Germans didn't succeed in their aim. The British people did not push for surrender, just for better defence systems. Troops were called away from the fighting in Europe to set up defence systems in Britain and these systems made German losses too heavy for the raids to continue.

Wartime bombing: 1940–44

Britain was at war with Germany again from 1939 to 1945. Once again, Germany targeted British civilians for much the same reasons as before.

This time German planes and bombs were more powerful, so bombing was more widespread and more destructive. The Germans had many more planes that could fly further and carry more bombs. In wave after wave of raids, about 62,000 British civilians were killed and about 200,000 wounded. Homes and whole town centres in target towns and cities were badly hit. People were often without water, gas or electricity. Roads were bombed or blocked with rubble; this disrupted bus, train and tram services. Sometimes streets were so blocked it was difficult to even walk or cycle to work.

Again, civilians did not push for surrender – instead they prided themselves on carrying on as normal. Government propaganda suggested everyone in was cheerfully going about their business. This was an exaggeration, but many people said the bombing made them determined to keep going.

Helping hand

When you answer a question about continuity, remember that nothing ever stays completely the same. You must consider things that have stayed the same, but also things that have changed, and make it clear in your answer that you have done this.

Don't say, *'there was continuity, the Germans bombed civilians in both wars'*.

Do say, *'there was continuity, the Germans bombed civilians in both wars. But the damage done in the Second World War was far greater'*.

Don't give examples of minor differences that do not affect the answer, such as the clothes people are wearing in the source photos.

Activity

2. a) Think about civilians as targets in the First and Second World Wars. Make a list of things that show continuity.

    b) Make a list of things that are different.

3. Draw a balance scale that shows how your two lists balance off against each other. Label one side 'change' and the other side 'continuity'. You will need to decide how balanced the sides are. Are there about the same number for each side or more for one side? Make sure you draw the tilt of your balance to show this.

Source B: A street in the East End of London after a bombing raid in April 1941.

Peacetime bombing: the IRA

The Irish Republican Army (IRA) was one of many groups that wanted to put pressure on the British government to let the Irish govern themselves. The IRA saw themselves as 'at war', so their tactics included bombing. IRA bombings in Britain came in waves. From 1969, when the British sent troops into Northern Ireland, IRA bombing increased.

The IRA campaign of protests and bombings were different from German wartime bombing because they lasted far longer. The IRA bombings were also different because they were not mass bombings of cities from the air, but smaller-scale bombings of single targets. But the IRA and Germany both used bombs and both targeted civilians.

A big difference between the IRA and German bombing was that the IRA gave the police warnings about bombs they had planted. They publicised this, saying they gave enough time for the police to clear the area. They were trying to keep public support by making the police, not themselves, seem responsible for deaths caused by the bombs. The warnings had an added advantage for the IRA: they caused disruption not casualties. Bomb warnings for railway and Underground stations, for example, cause a lot of disruption.

The IRA bombing and the German bombing were intended to make people fearful and to cause a lot of disruption, to pressure the British government to act in a particular way. Both caused disruption and both made people fearful. German bombing did not make the public press for surrender, but was the IRA bombing more persuasive?

Public opinion about the IRA's campaign was more divided than it was over surrendering to Germany. A large number of people supported the idea of the Irish governing themselves. Even more supported the idea of taking British troops out of Northern Ireland after 1969. However, the IRA bombing campaigns didn't seem to bring the IRA more public support, even though they stressed they did not want a lot of casualties. Instead, it lost them sympathy for using bombing as a tactic at all.

Source C: Canary Wharf, near the East End of London, after an IRA bomb exploded there in February 1996.

A different kind of bombing: 2005

On the morning of 7 July 2005, four bombs exploded in Central London. Three were on Underground trains; the fourth was on a bus. The bombing resembled IRA bombing in several ways:

- Civilians were targeted.

- There was a wave of incidents, or suspected incidents.

- The effects were similar. People died and were injured. There was a lot of publicity. Security measures were at a heightened state.

- The bombers saw themselves as 'at war'. In a video recording found after the bombing, one of them called himself 'a soldier' and 'at war'.

However, they were also different from IRA bombings.

- There was no warning, no time to clear the area. The bombers intended to kill people – as many as possible. The IRA often gave warnings in order to cause disruption not casualties.

- The bombers, four British Muslims, were suicide bombers. While members of the IRA had been killed in some explosions, it was accidental, due to bombs exploding too soon.

- While they saw themselves as 'at war', as did the IRA, the 2005 bombers' war was global (against western ideas and values), not just anti-British.

Did you know?

The news coverage of the 7 July 2005 bombings used images from mobile phones – both of people caught in the Underground explosions, and of people outside.

Making a judgement

Various groups targeted civilians during the 20th century, often using bombs, to try to make governments act in a certain way. From the evidence of this lesson, how far do you think they achieved their aims?

Source D: The site of the London bus bomb under police investigation on 11 July 2005.

Activity

4. Match the heads and tails below to make three sentences about continuity.

Heads	Tails
Continuity is how things	both continuity and change.
Historians must consider	stay the same over time.
Things very seldom	stay exactly the same.

5. Make a continuity balance scale for peacetime bombing, in the same way as you did for wartime bombing on page 29.

Impact

1.7 The impact of television on daily life

32

Lesson objectives

By the end of this lesson, you should be able to:
* explain some of the ways in which TV has made an impact on everyday life in Britain
* understand how to analyse impact
* consider the factors that affect how much impact something has.

When historians consider the impact of an invention or event they have to consider how many people used or were affected by it and how widespread the effects were. You are going to consider the impact of television on daily life in Britain.

Activity

1. As you read through the examples of the impact of TV, make notes about how you think the impact might be affected by:
   * the availability of TV
   * the number of different channels
   * what is broadcast on TV
   * the possibility of recording (and so re-timing) TV programmes.

Early television

In 1956 a survey of television ownership found that 36 per cent of homeowners had a TV. But they only had two channels and the picture was in black and white. By 2010, 97 per cent of homeowners had at least one TV. Many channels could be watched and the picture was in colour. All through the 20th century, television grew. It broadcast for more hours of the day, had more channels and developed different types of programmes. As all these things happened, TV had an impact on the way that people behaved. As TV changed, so did the impact that it had.

Source A: UK television ownership 1949-2000.

Year	Homes with TVs
1947	15,000
1950	344,000
1960	10,470,000
1970	16,316,000
1980	18,522,000
1990	21,311,000
2000	24,265,000

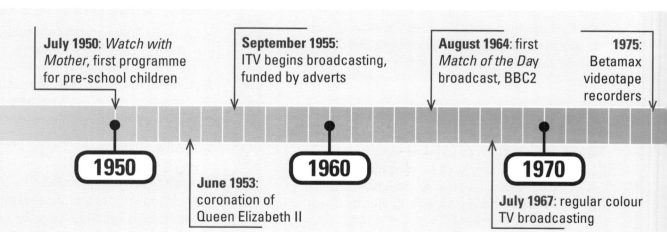

July 1950: *Watch with Mother*, first programme for pre-school children

September 1955: ITV begins broadcasting, funded by adverts

August 1964: first *Match of the Day* broadcast, BBC2

1975: Betamax videotape recorders

1950

1960

1970

June 1953: coronation of Queen Elizabeth II

July 1967: regular colour TV broadcasting

World view

1963: assassination of President Kennedy in the USA shows how TV brought particular world events closer

1969: US series *Sesame Street* for pre-school viewers first shown

Families

- watching and talking about TV together
- seeing other kinds of families
- eating in front of TV together – TV dinners became widely available in the late 1960s

Entertainment

- less going to the cinema
- less going to football matches

Education

1957: TV broadcasts for schools begin

Impact of TV on daily life 1950–70

Social issues

1966: *Cathy Come Home* highlights problems of homelessness

Working lives

- talking about TV programmes
- new jobs

Travel

1950: first cross-channel broadcast from Paris. First of many 'tastes' of Europe to encourage travel

Culture

1964: *Top of the Pops* gives huge boost to record sales

- Fashion trends spread fast and country-wide

Helping hand

When asked about the impact of something, be sure to check 'impact on who or what'. For example, for TV to have an impact on Britain there needs to be a reasonable number of televisions in British homes. Only then will enough people be affected for it to have a country-wide impact. When you talk about this kind of impact you have to make generalisations. Nothing affects everyone in a country in the same way. Use phrases such as '*many people*' or '*some people*' in your answers from time to time, to show you don't think everyone was affected, or affected in the same way.

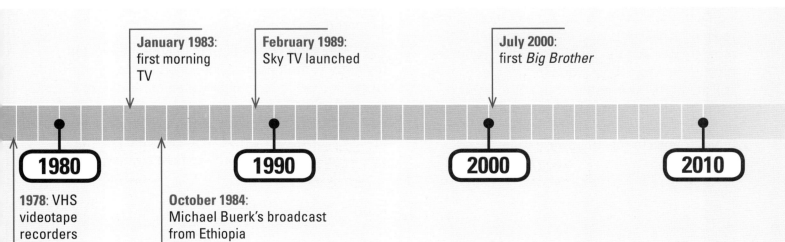

January 1983: first morning TV

February 1989: Sky TV launched

July 2000: first *Big Brother*

1980

1990

2000

2010

1978: VHS videotape recorders

October 1984: Michael Buerk's broadcast from Ethiopia

Impact on general behaviour

In the 1950s and 1960s, many people went out for entertainment: to the cinema; to football matches and to other sporting events. Cinemas and sports grounds made a lot of money from admission tickets and sales of food, drink and other goods. But as more homes got TV, attendance at sports grounds and cinemas dropped. People stayed at home to watch the sport, the films or other TV.

In the 1960s and 1970s some shows were so popular that almost everyone watched them, and talked about them at school and at work the next day. They started to use 'catchphrases', from these shows in conversation that were lost on people who hadn't seen the show.

Source B: UK cinema attendance 1950–2009.

Year	Cinema attendance
1950	1,395,800,000
1960	500,800,000
1970	193,000,000
1980	101,000,000
1990	96,000,000
2000	143,000,000
2009	173,500,000

Impact on family behaviour

In the 1950s and 60s, most families only had one TV. They sat together in the main room to watch it, and they could only watch one channel. But by the end of the 1980s falling prices meant that a growing number of families had more than one TV – a TV in the main room and one or more in other rooms. People could now choose to watch different programmes and the family began to spend less time in the same room watching TV. Many people still ate in front of the TV – but not together. Some ate the same meal at the same time, but in different rooms. Some ate TV dinners at different times, thanks to the microwave oven.

Impact on attitudes

As TV developed, BBC and ITV both started broadcasting 'soaps' – long running serials with several storylines that followed the same groups of people over time. These became very popular. The highest rated began to run several times a week rather than once. TV channels began to use 'Christmas' editions of soaps to attract viewers.

ITV's most successful long-running soap is *Coronation Street*. The most successful soap of all is *EastEnders*, on BBC. As soaps became more and more talked about, they started to develop storylines about issues such as racism, single parenting, alcoholism and drug use. The *EastEnders* website now has a special webpage with links for people who have been affected by any issues in the programme.

Impact on interests

TV has always had education programmes for schools. However, it has also educated people in other ways. It has given them a more global view of the world through travel programmes. It has produced documentaries that teach, for example, about wildlife, the stars and planets or history.

Because TV reached so many people, it had a big impact (as it does now) if it raised issues that gripped the country. Two examples of this are the 1966 TV drama *Cathy Come Home* and the 1984 news report on the famine in Ethiopia. *Cathy Come Home* was a TV drama about homelessness. It was a play, but showed real problems faced by homeless people in Britain. Viewers were shocked by what they saw. The homeless charity Shelter was set up at this time and had a lot of public support due to the TV drama.

The 1984 report on the famine in Ethiopia brought the famine into Britain's living rooms. It led to the singer Bob Geldof persuading many music stars to perform for free on a 'Band Aid' record rushed out for Christmas. It made £8 million. Geldof set up Live Aid, a charity that organised concerts over several years to raise money to fight poverty.

Source C: The Live Aid concert at Wembley 13 July 1985.

More choice, less impact?

During the 1980s video recorders became more widespread allowing people to record TV programmes to watch at a later time. In 1989, Sky TV was launched in Britain, providing many more channels. In 1998 Sky went digital; new technology allowed them to broadcast hundreds of channels, and in 2001 they introduced Sky Plus. This let viewers record the programmes they wanted to watch, simply and easily, with links to series; once the series link was set up, the viewer didn't have to remember to do any recording. The impact of TV programmes is not the same as when there were only two channels, and almost everyone watched the same popular programmes.

Digital TV has also expanded into on-demand TV. People can now watch some TV on computers or other digital equipment. Not being tied to a time or place has had a huge impact on when and where people watch TV, and what else they do with their leisure time. Some think that this has led to the rise in the number of people going to the cinema (see Source B).

Activity

2. Copy the timeline from pages 32–33, putting in additional important dates from the text.

3. Write a flyer for a new digital TV provider. Pick the two benefits of digital TV that you think are most important and use these in your flyer. Use as few words as possible – make every word count!

4. Write a paragraph about what impact a TV programme could have in the 1960s, and now. Do you think the increase in the number of TV channels and the ability to watch programmes at any time means that programmes have a greater or lesser impact now?

5. Draw a diagram like the one on page 33 to show the impact of TV 1970-2010. Don't forget to think about the impact of new types of TV (such as reality shows).

Making a judgement

1.8 Are we healthier now than in 1900?

Lesson objectives

By the end of this lesson, you should be able to:
- understand health issues in 1900 and now
- weigh up the evidence on both sides of a question
- make a judgement on a question.

This lesson focuses on how we make a judgement about something. This involves assessing information provided to consider a question, and to reach your own judgement on the question, using evidence from the information. You will be looking at whether people are healthier in Britain now than in 1900.

Factors making us healthier

There have been various advances since 1900 that have made people in Britain healthier.

- Medical practice has improved. In 1900, operating theatres were clean, but not sterile (as they are now). People did not wear masks to prevent infection.

- The NHS (set up in 1948) now provides much of our medical care, free of charge. In 1900 you had to pay for your medical care or medicines, or do without.

- State **unemployment benefit** (set up in 1911) now gives many people financial help. So fewer people now get ill due to being underfed.

- Improvements in science and technology have allowed the development of machines that help diagnose disease and to cure it. Surgeons now use new equipment, such as lasers. New drugs also fight and prevent disease.

- **Public health services** have improved. Almost all people now have clean piped water, toilets and rubbish collection – many more than in 1900.

- Changes in fuels used in homes and factories mean that the air is cleaner than in 1900.

Factors making us less healthy

Our lives are very different from those of people in 1900. Lifestyles have improved in some ways, but

- we get less exercise. In 1900 many people regularly walked miles to work or school each day. Today, more people rely on cars (there are no figures for 1900, but as late as 1950 only 14% of homes had a car), and on public transport.

- More people also had jobs that involved exercise in 1900. They were more active in their free time, too. Now, with centrally heated homes and a wide range of home entertainment from TV and computers, we are more likely to stay indoors.

- we eat more processed food. In 1900 you could not buy ready meals or the wide variety of fast- and snack food (or fizzy drinks) that we can buy now. These foods often have high levels of both fat and sugar.

- many people have more money to spend. Since 1900, wages have risen four times higher than prices. More people can afford to spend money on snack food, alcohol and tobacco (all bad for your health in excess) than in 1900.

Now you have looked at the facts, examine the various areas of health below to see how our health now compares to health in 1900.

Activity

1. As you work through the sources and information, make two lists: one of examples of how we are healthier now and one of examples of how we are not healthier now.

Who gets sick most?

The least healthy people in 1900 were the poor. Poor families were large, and crowded together into houses which often had no running water or toilets. Sewage and rubbish were often just dumped in the streets. People frequently didn't get enough food or fuel.

In these conditions, diseases such as cholera and typhoid (carried in dirty water) spread quickly, as did **infectious** childhood diseases, such as measles and whooping cough. Tuberculosis (TB), an infectious lung disease, killed about 80,000 people in 1900. These diseases came in epidemic waves and, because they were all infectious, killed more people in the poorest, most crowded areas.

State benefits mean that most poor people now have better living conditions. The development of vaccines and the introduction of NHS care have reduced the death rate from infectious diseases sharply (in 2004, about 340 people died from TB). However, poor people still have the worst living and working conditions and remain the least healthy sector of society in Britain. The death rate for all diseases is still highest among the poor, and highest of all among the homeless.

Source A: From a book published in 1988 about social change in Britain since 1900.

Infant mortality from infectious diseases and TB has been almost eliminated. … This has been an important cause in the changing life expectation at various ages. The life expectation of the young has risen by over 20 years since 1900.

Glossary

infectious: easily passed from one person to another by touch or breath

unemployment benefit: a weekly amount paid by the state to people qualifying for the payment and who cannot find work

public health services: services that improve the general health of everyone in the country: such as mains drainage, rubbish removal, clean water

Source B: An operation in a London hospital in 1900.

Surviving childhood

In 1900, many babies, and their mothers, died in childbirth. If a baby survived, 154 of every 1000 died before their first birthday. Babies and young children were vulnerable to diseases that often proved fatal. This meant that the longer a child lived the better its chance of survival into old age (Source C).

Since 1900, medical advances (vaccination, antibiotics and access to care) and better living conditions have increased the survival rate for babies at birth and in their first year. They have also reduced deaths from childhood diseases, such as whooping cough or measles. Life expectancy from birth to the age of 15 has improved (Source C).

Living longer

People live longer now than they did in 1900. But many of these extra years of life are affected by diseases that give a poor quality of life. These diseases can be physical (cancer, heart disease) or mental (Alzheimer's disease). People who collect information about life expectancy, now measure healthy life expectancy (HLE) too. This is measured as the ability to have a reasonable quality of life and being free of life-affecting disease. In 2007 women had a life expectancy of 82. Their HLE was 65. Male life expectancy in 2007 was 78, their HLE was 63.

Source D: A knee operation in January 2010. The screens show what the surgeon is doing.

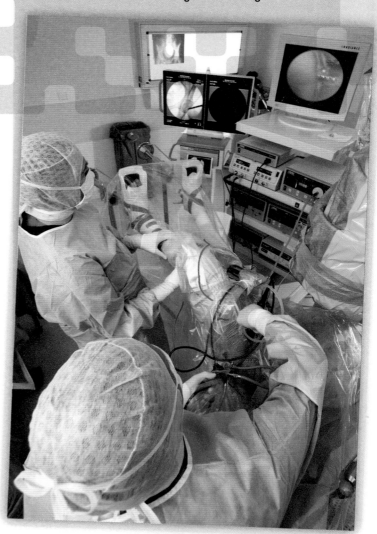

Source C: Life expectation for babies born in the UK, and in later life, for 1900 and 2007, from government statistics.

Sex and age of baby	1900	2007
male		
birth	46	78
1 year	57	78
15 years	62	78
female		
birth	52	82
1 year	59	82
15 years	62	82

Helping hand

When you are making a judgement about something, you are usually trying to work out how important something was, how far you agree with a statement, or if one particular cause was the main cause of an event.

In all these cases, you must balance the evidence for and against and then give a judgement, which you need to explain. You also need to give as much detail as you can to support your statement.

Don't just say, *fewer babies die at birth now than in 1900.*

Do say, *In 1900, of all babies born alive, 154 of every thousand died before reaching their first birthday. In 2009 it was 4 out of every thousand.*

38

Different diseases

The diseases that people suffer from, and those that they die from, have changed since 1900.

- There are fewer epidemics (waves of infectious diseases); fewer people die of these diseases when they catch them. About a third of deaths in 1900 were from epidemics; in 1997 it was about a sixth.

- Fewer people have the kinds of breathing diseases brought on by working conditions (for example, miners breathing coal dust). Now, more people have back problems brought on by desk work.

- In 1900 the biggest single cause of death was infectious disease, and it killed mostly young people. Now the biggest single cause of death is cancer, which accounts for over 40 per cent of all deaths. The reason for this is partly because we are more able to detect it and so know it is cancer that causes the deaths, partly because we are living longer (so have more chance to get it), and partly because the way we live makes us more likely to get it.

- More people now have 'lifestyle' diseases – diseases produced by the way they live. Obesity (being greatly overweight) is on the rise because we now take less exercise and eat more fatty foods. Obesity can contribute to various other diseases, and puts a significant strain on the heart. Smoking makes it more likely that people may get cancer and also that they will have blood circulation problems. Drinking too much alcohol makes liver diseases more likely.

Source E: From a government report on changes in the UK 1900–1997, published in 1999.

The age of death has changed significantly. In 1911–15, 63 per cent of all deaths were 'premature' (under 60 years old). In 1991–95, 12 per cent of deaths were of people under the age of 60.

Helping hand

When you are answering any question, read it carefully and work out exactly what is being asked. Take the question 'Are we healthier now than in 1900?'. You are being asked about comparing health generally in 1900, and now. You are not being asked if people live longer now, or if they have better medical care, although both might come into your answer.

Activity

You are going to plan an answer to the question 'Are we healthier now than in 1900?'.

Take the planning step by step.

1. Read the question carefully. You are going to compare the health of people in 1900, and now.

2. Read the lists you have made, of the ways we are healthier/less healthy than in 1900. Make sure your lists have covered:
   - medical advances
   - care available and what it cost
   - living conditions
   - lifestyle factors.

   Think about these and reach a judgement. Write a sentence or two saying what you think. Don't go into detail. Just say, *I think … because, as I will show, …*

3. Write your first paragraph about the evidence you have that suggests people are healthier. Start your paragraph, *On the one hand…*. Make sure you give evidence for each point you make.

4. Write your next paragraph about the evidence you have that suggests people are not healthier. Start your paragraph, *On the other hand…*. Make sure you give evidence for each point you make.

5. Now sum up the evidence and re-state your judgement. Remember to give as much relevant detail as you can. Use phrases such as, *In some ways we are healthier/unhealthier now because…* and *The evidence shows that…*

Source skills

Introduction

Lesson objectives

By the end of this lesson, you should be able to:

- understand the importance of annotating sources and using contextual knowledge
- make use of the contents of sources
- make use of the nature, origins and purpose of sources.

You will need to a use a variety of skills in order to answer source questions. These include: annotating sources, making use of the contents of sources, and understanding and being able to apply the nature, origins and purpose of sources.

Source questions

You will have to answer a variety of source questions including:

- making supported inferences
- identifying and explaining the message and purpose of a source
- cross-referencing/comparing sources
- explaining the usefulness of a source or sources
- using sources to test a view (hypothesis) of an event or person.

Contextual knowledge

This means the knowledge that you have about a topic or event. This knowledge will help you with your source skills because:

- It will ensure that you understand what the source is suggesting.
- It enables you to make judgements about the source itself – how accurate is it, and how well has it covered the event.

Contents

This is the information which the source gives you about an event or person. You will need to identify information such as dates and actual events as well as opinions and points of view. In addition, you should apply your contextual knowledge to answer several questions about the source:

- How well has the source covered an event? Has it left out important developments?
- Is the source giving a one-sided view? If so, which view is not being given?
- Is it accurate in its portrayal of the event?

Reliability

You will be asked to judge the reliability of sources. This means deciding how far you can trust the source. You can test reliability by:

- Checking the contents and information of the source against what you know about the event. Does it give an accurate view? Is anything missed out? For example the propaganda poster (Source A) is reliable in that some mothers were tempted to return to towns and cities. It is less reliable because not all evacuees lived in the pleasant conditions shown.
- Examining the Nature, Origins and Purpose of the source. Can you fully trust who produced the source? Are they giving you a one-sided, exaggerated or even distorted view in order to get your support? For example the poster is a reliable view of the propaganda used by the British government during the Second World War but exaggerates the influence of Hitler in order to get across its message.

The Nature, Origins and Purpose of sources (NOP)

This tests your ability to make use of the provenance of the source.

NOP	Questions to ask	Examples
Nature	What type of source is it? Is it a cartoon, photograph, painting, speech, diary, newspaper article? What difference does this make?	A diary often gives a very personal view A photograph often gives a very limited view of what took place A cartoon often gives an exaggerated view of a person or event
Origins	When was the source produced – at the time or later? What difference does this make? Who produced the source? What do you know about him or her? Will this make it a one-sided view of the person or event?	Eyewitness accounts provide first hand evidence of the event or person but can give a limited and even distorted account. Accounts written later often have the benefit of hindsight but can lack a feel for that event. Here you can apply your contextual knowledge. Remember that one-side accounts are useful in that they give you a particular view of the event or person.
Purpose	Why was the source produced? What is it trying to make you think or do? Which side is it trying to get you to support? Who is it trying to turn you against?	Speeches are made to get you to support a person or group. Cartoons are often produced to poke fun at people or events. Posters are often produced as propaganda.

Source A: A British government poster from 1942, about evacuation.

Key details

Ghost-like figure of Hitler, tempting the mother. Mother and children in the countryside. Mother looks unsure.

Nature

A poster. Posters are usually produced for propaganda purposes to give a message to persuade people to think or act in a certain way.

Origins

It was produced in 1942, during the Second World War, when there was much less German bombing of British cities than in earlier years of the war. It was produced by the British government, who used posters for propaganda purposes.

Contextual knowledge

The poster is about evacuation. By 1942, there was little bombing of British cities, and many children and mothers had returned from evacuation to town and city centres.

Purpose

It was a propaganda poster to convince mothers and their children to remain in the countryside, and not return to the town or city centres.

Comprehension/inference

2.1 Conscientious objectors

42

Lesson objectives

By the end of this lesson, you should be able to:

- understand what some people thought about conscientious objectors
- understand how they were treated
- comprehend a source and summarise key points
- make supported inferences.

Helping hand

Comprehension

You may be asked to summarise important points of information from a source. For example, 'What does Source A tell you about why Clifford Allen refused to join up?'

An example has been shown for Source A.

In this section you will learn how to use two important source skills: comprehension and inference. Comprehension means understanding the source and being able to summarise key points. Inference is the word to describe something that, although not actually stated or shown in the source, can be worked out from it.

Conscientious objectors

As you saw in section 1.1, during the First World War there were some men who refused to join up and fight for their country. These conscientious objectors were often more hated than the enemy and in some cases, suffered a worse fate than the British soldiers in the trenches. We will be looking at what people thought of conscientious objectors and how they were treated.

In 1916 the government introduced conscription, due to huge losses on the **Western Front**. Approximately 16,000 men refused to join the army because they were conscientious objectors. Men who wanted to be excused from military service had to appear before a military court to give their reasons for being excused.

- Some eventually agreed to join the army, and accepted non-fighting roles such as medical orderlies, stretcher bearers and drivers.

- About 1,500 – known as **absolutists** – refused to join the army and follow any sort of military orders. Absolutists were sent to military camps.

Source A: From the evidence given in 1916 by Clifford Allen, a conscientious objector, to a military tribunal.

> Source A tells me that Clifford Allen refused to join up because he wanted peace

> I believe that you sitting here and the people of all nations on both sides want peace. I believe that it is the fault of the governments that this has not happened. I will not take part in any war which I believe could be stopped immediately. I resist war because I love freedom. Conscription is a denial of freedom. You can shut me up in prison over and over again, but you cannot imprison my free spirit.

> Source A also tells me that Clifford Allen believed in freedom and that conscription went against his belief in freedom

What did people think of conscientious objectors?

Although some support was given to conscientious objectors by organisations such as the No-Conscription Fellowship, for the most part they were treated as cowards, traitors or criminals by the majority of people. White feathers, which were a symbol of cowardice, were handed out to young men who had not joined the army. Families and friends would have nothing to do with them. They were treated like outcasts (see pages 9–10).

Strangely enough, many soldiers at home and fighting in the trenches admired the conscientious objectors and realised that, in many ways, it was braver to stand up for one's beliefs and go against the views of the majority.

Moreover, those that performed non-fighting duties were often sent to the front as stretcher-bearers. Here they faced the same risks as all the other troops, and sometimes worse. For example, they carried wounded men back from no-man's land – the churned up area between the two trench systems on the Western Front.

Source B: John Graham, a **Quaker**, explains reactions to conscientious objectors during the First World War.

'The conscientious objector seemed to most people to be merely a shirker. He was shunned by the women he knew. His mother and brothers jeered at him at home. He was called a "shirker", "coward" or "dog". People shouted "you are only fit to be on the end of a German bayonet".'

Another inference could be that they were very unpopular. This is shown when the source says people shouted that 'you are only fit to be on the end of a German bayonet'.

Helping hand

Inference

In history we often try to squeeze more information from a source than it actually tells us. For example, we like to know how people felt about big events, as well as knowing what actually happened. In other words, we make inferences from sources.

This is more than just understanding and summarising the key points of a source. You are being asked to read between the lines of a source – to explain what it is suggesting. What is its attitude or tone? Is the writer sarcastic, sad, pleased, angry, happy, supportive, determined etc.? The inference can be about the situation described in the source, or about the message that the author or artist wants to convey.

We often draw inferences about people from their body language. For example, a student yawns during a history lesson. One inference could be that the student is bored with the lesson. Another inference could be the student is tired, possibly due to a late night.

You will need to support any inferences with evidence from the source. With a written source, this could be directly quoting or paraphrasing from the source.

One inference could be that conscientious objectors were treated as outcasts. This is supported when Source B says 'He was shunned by the women he knew.' or 'His mother and brothers jeered at him at home.'

Glossary

absolutist: conscientious objector who refused to do any military duties including non-fighting duties

Quaker: a member of a religious group, known as the Society of Friends

Western Front: area of the trench system in France and Belgium where most of the fighting took place during the First World War

43

44

Source C: Percy Wall, a conscientious objector, describes the reactions of some soldiers.

The attitude of the soldiers at the work camp varied. A very small minority told us they would like to see us shot. Others wished to know exactly what we were standing for and some of them told us they would be conscientious objectors next time. Another group seemed to think we were simply trying to get out of the trenches.'

Activity

1. What does Source C tell you about reactions to conscientious objectors? See if you can give at least two reactions.

Helping hand

You will be asked to make inferences from illustrations such as cartoons, posters, paintings and photographs. Examine closely the details of the Source D illustration, as well as the information given about the source. These will help you to work out the source message, or messages.

Source D: A cartoon which was published in a magazine in May 1918. The caption on the cartoon read 'This little pig stayed at home'.

The cartoon shows members of the man's family each doing important war work. The inference could be that the cartoon's message is that he is letting down his family.

One inference could be that conscientious objectors were attacked in the press, as the cartoon was published in a magazine

The conscientious objector is shown sitting in a seat doing nothing and smoking. The inference could be that the cartoon's message is that he is idle, and doing nothing to help with the war effort.

How were conscientious objectors treated?

The government found it impossible to persuade employers to take on those conscientious objectors who were prepared to carry out civilian work not linked directly to the war effort and, from June 1916, set up Home Office Work Centres. Here the conditions were often very harsh. At one centre in Dyce, near Aberdeen, the men were forced to live in tents and conditions were so cold and harsh that several died of pneumonia. These work centres remained open until April 1919, six months after the war ended, by which time 73 conscientious objectors had died.

The absolutists suffered the worst treatment. They were given no sympathy by the military courts and were sent to prison camps. Some were beaten, kept in solitary confinement in filthy cells, and given uncooked food. Men were suspended by their wrists from a rope so their feet dangled over the ground. Others were put in wooden cages like animals. Some were thrown naked into sewage ponds.

Source E: Howard Marten, an absolutist, describes his treatment.

'We were placed in handcuffs and locked in the cells and tied up for two hours in the afternoon. We were tied by the wrists to horizontal ropes about five feet off the ground with our arms outstretched and our feet tied together. Then we were confined to our cells for three days on "punishment diet", which consisted of four biscuits a day and water. We were also handcuffed with our hands behind us. Rats were frequent visitors to our cells.

Did you know?

The prison cells of Richmond Castle, in North Yorkshire, were used to hold conscientious objectors. On the walls of the cells there is graffiti drawn by prisoners who were held there.

Activity

2. Give two examples of the harsh treatment of conscientious objectors.

3. You have seen how we often make inferences about people from their body language. Working in pairs, one strike a certain pose or make a facial expression whilst the other makes an inference from it.

4. Study Source E. What can you learn from Source E about the treatment of conscientious objectors? See if you can make at least two inferences, supported from the source.

Making a judgement

There were two very different views about conscientious objectors during the First World War. The majority thought they were cowards and were betraying their country. However, a minority believed they showed even greater bravery than those who joined up. What evidence could you use from this section to support the two different views and what is your own judgement?

Message and purpose

2.2 Government reactions to the suffragettes

46

Lesson objectives

By the end of this lesson, you should be able to:
- understand government reactions to the **suffragettes**
- analyse written and visual sources to work out how an event or person is portrayed
- identify and explain the message and purpose of a source

One important skill is the ability to analyse details of a source in order to work out how an event or person is portrayed. To fully use a source you will need to understand what its message and overall purpose is.

Helping hand

When analysing a source, think about it in the same way that you think about taking a photograph. To get the effect you want, you choose which things to focus on and which ones to leave out. When you analyse a source, break it into sections and look at each part separately in order to see what impression the artist or author is trying to make. With written sources, examine the following:
- the language; the words used by the author
- the views or arguments put forward
- what overall message does the source give.

An example, looking at Source A, has been done for you

Source A: From a book written in 1907, called *Woman or Suffragette* by Marie Corelli.

The use of language to turn people against the suffragettes, *'"Votes for women" is the shrill cry of a number of discontented ladies.'*

' "Votes for women" is the shrill cry of a number of discontented ladies. But the truth is that Women were and are destined to make voters rather than to be voters themselves. It cannot be denied that women suffer great injustice at the hands of men. But this is the result of the way in which mothers have reared their sons and still continue to rear them.'

She chooses her reason for opposing votes for women – their domestic role, *'But the truth is that Women were and are destined to make voters rather than to be voters themselves.'*

She emphasises that the men who mistreat women are those who have not been brought up properly by their mothers who have neglected their domestic role, *'But this is the result of the way in which mothers have reared their sons and still continue to rear them.'*

Message

Overall, the source suggests that a woman should not be involved in votes for women, as their role is to produce and bring up children.

Suffragette militancy

In the years before the First World War, the extreme activities of the suffragettes, which often included breaking the law, made front page news.

The Women's Political and Social Union (WSPU), led by Emily and Christabel Pankhurst, was the most famous group that campaigned for the vote at the beginning of the 20th century. These women were nicknamed the suffragettes, and believed that the peaceful methods of campaigning for the vote used by the suffragists – such as petitions and marches – were not effective (see pages 12–15). They were prepared to carry out more **militant** methods in order to get publicity and force the government to act. For example:

- In March 1912 they started a massive stone-throwing campaign in the centre of London, with the police arresting 219 suffragettes.

- They set fire to post boxes, bombed churches and damaged cricket pitches and golf courses.

- They slashed valuable paintings in art galleries, cut telephone wires and set fire to derelict buildings.

However there was considerable opposition to the activities of the suffragettes, from men and from women.

Helping hand

If you look at a picture source – for example a poster or cartoon – you need to think about the following:

- what details have been included and why
- what the centre of attention is and how the artist has made it the centre of attention
- whether anything has been deliberately missed out.

These details will help you to work out how the artist has portrayed the event or person, and the message that is trying to be conveyed. See the analysis of Source B for an example.

Glossary

militant: prepared to use extreme methods to get a result

Activity

1. Study Source B. How does the poster portray the actions of the suffragettes? What is the message of this source?

Source B: A poster published in 1912 by the National League for Opposing Women's Suffrage. The small note says 'Back in an hour or so'.

To emphasise that the wife and mother is a suffragette. However, no mention of the reasons why women wanted the vote.

Two children feature in the centre of the poster. They both look neglected and unhappy.

Husband of the suffragette who looks shocked at what he comes home to after doing a hard day's work.

Shows that housework is being neglected by the mother because of her suffragette activities.

Hunger striking and forced feeding

More and more suffragettes were arrested and put in prison. In 1909 one suffragette, Marion Wallace-Dunlop, who was serving a prison sentence, refused to eat food and was released within a few days. The WSPU now decided to use this tactic of hunger striking.

The prison authorities, who were afraid that a suffragette might die in prison, thus giving them even more publicity, introduced forced-feeding. This was carried out for the first time on a suffragette, Mary Leigh, who had been imprisoned for throwing slates through the roof at a meeting where Asquith, the Prime Minister, was speaking. Meat juice and lime cordial were dripped into her stomach through a tube down her throat.

Forced feeding became a standard way of treating suffragettes on hunger strike. Usually, the tube was pushed down the throat, but if the victim resisted, the tube would be pushed into her stomach through her nose. Hunger strikers were given a medical inspection by a doctor, to make sure that they were fit enough for the process.

48

Helping hand

You may be asked to explain why a source was produced, in other words its purpose. In order to do this you need to:

- Examine the details of the source and use these to work out the message of the source — what it is suggesting. Use your inference skills from section 2.1.
- Make a careful note of the information given about the source: who produced it and when. This will help you to identify its purpose.
- Finally, explain the purpose of the source. Purpose means what is the source trying to make people at the time think or do. Is it trying to get support, or to turn people against the event, person, group etc.?
- Use details from the source and your own contextual knowledge, to support the message and purpose.

Source C: A WSPU poster from 1909 showing forced feeding.

Message

The source suggests that forced feeding was an horrific and painful experience. Look at the number of people holding the captive down, and the cruel look on the face of the wardresses. The suffragette looks in agony and is having her leg tied.

Purpose

This was produced by the WSPU to win support for the suffragette cause for votes for women, and to turn people against the Liberal Government, at a time when many suffragettes were being force-fed. The health of some suffragettes, such as Lady Constance Lytton, was badly affected by forced feeding. It was also meant to win sympathy for the suffering of the suffragettes, and to put pressure on the Liberals to stop forced feeding.

Did you know?

Lady Constance Lytton was arrested the first time for throwing a stone at the car of a leading Liberal. She went on hunger strike but was released after a medical examination showed that her heart was too weak to stand up to the strain of forced feeding, but also because her family were wealthy. When she was later re-arrested, she gave a different name, Jane Wharton, and was force-fed several times, without having been medically examined. This brought about a stroke which left her partially paralysed.

The 'Cat & Mouse Act', 1913

By 1913 the Liberal government realised it needed a different method of dealing with hunger striking. Forced feeding had brought very bad publicity for the Liberal government.

In 1913, Asquith introduced the Temporary Discharge Act. This allowed hunger strikers to leave prison, recover a little and then return to finish their sentences. Licenses for release usually allowed a week's freedom before re-arrest. Emily Pankhurst, whilst serving a three-sentence prison sentence, was let out so frequently that one journalist calculated in 1913 that she would not serve all her sentence until 1930!

The suffragettes nicknamed this the 'Cat and Mouse Act'. It brought bad publicity for the Liberal government and yet more sympathy for the suffragettes.

Source D: From a speech in May 1913 by Keir Hardie, the leader of the Labour Party, about the Cat and Mouse Act.

'The Temporary Discharge Bill is unnecessary, harsh and cruel even for the purpose for which it was intended. We believed that the government was seeking an alternative to forcible feeding. What they are offering is not such an alternative but simply additional powers to the authorities in the use of forcible feeding. The licenses for release might double, triple or quadruple the length of the original jail sentence given to the suffragette.'

Activity

2. Give one reason why the government:

   a) force-fed the suffragettes

   b) introduced the Cat and Mouse Act.

3. Study Source B. What was the purpose of this poster? Remember to identify and explain the message and purpose of the source, using details from the source and your contextual knowledge.

4. Study Source D. How does Keir Hardie portray the Cat and Mouse Act and what message is he giving out?

5. In what ways do you think the actions of the suffragettes and the government helped or hindered the cause of votes for women? Make a copy of the following scales and on the left hand side list those actions that helped, and on the right side list those that hindered.

Making a judgement

The Liberal government used two different approaches in dealing with the problem of suffragette prisoners who went on hunger strike: forced feeding and invoking the 'Cat and Mouse Act'. Which do you think was:

- the most cruel
- the most effective?

Give reasons for your answers.

49

Cross-referencing

50 2.3 Propaganda during the Second World War

Lesson objectives

By the end of this lesson, you should be able to:
- describe different methods used by the government for propaganda during the Second World War
- understand how to cross-reference – compare and contrast sources.

Helping hand

One way to cross-reference sources is to highlight in one colour, areas of agreement between the sources and in a different colour, areas of disagreement.
- Highlight in green any areas of support in what the sources suggest.
- Highlight in red any areas of challenge between the sources.

One example of each from Sources A, B and C has been done for you on page 51.

Cross-referencing is a very important skill. We often compare two or more views of a sporting event, a pop concert or even a television programme. In this section you will see how to compare and contrast the views of different sources. You are going to cross-reference sources in the context of government methods of propaganda during the Second World War.

The radio

During the Second World War the British government used a variety of methods to keep up the morale of the British people and ensure that the war effort was supported. The Ministry of Information (MOI) was set up in September 1939 to organise propaganda, and used broadcasts and propaganda films to get across its message.

Almost nine million people owned radios in Britain at the outbreak of war, which meant that almost every family had access to one. Therefore, it became a very important method of involving the population and keeping them informed.

The BBC sent out news reporters to the battle fronts and they sent back reports of British forces in action, which were then broadcast the following day. One of the most controversial BBC broadcasts was given by Charles Gardner in July 1940, during the Battle of Britain when he described an attack by British fighter planes on German bombers.

However, there were mixed reactions to the broadcast. It was criticised by some for being too similar to a sports commentary, and not serious enough.

Part of Charles Gardner's broadcast, 14 July 1940.

'There's one going down in flames. Somebody's hit a German and he's coming down with a long streak — coming down completely out of control — a long streak of smoke — and now a man's baled out by parachute. The pilot's baled out by parachute. He's a Junkers 87, and he's going slap into the sea — and there he goes. SMASH! A terrific column of water and there was a Junkers 87. Only one man got out by parachute, so presumably there was only a crew of one in it.'

Glossary

dog-fight: a battle in the air between aircraft

Helping hand

Having compared Sources A, B and C, you must now make a final judgement. Ask yourself:

- Is there strong agreement or disagreement between Sources A and C and B and C?
- Is there some agreement and disagreement?

Use judgement words or phrases such as *strongly agree, strongly disagree, very little agreement, much agreement.*

Make a copy of the following grid and use it to help you plan your answer.

Sources	Agree	Disagree	Extent of support
A and C			
B and C			

Activity

1. You may be asked to compare or cross reference two or more sources. For example,

   How far do Sources A and B support the views of Source C about the broadcast by Charles Gardner?

   The information in the Helping Hand box will guide you through building your answer.

Source A: From an interview by a headmaster in Scotland to the Listener Research Section of the BBC in 1940.

Source B: From an article in the *Daily Telegraph*, the day after the views broadcast in Source A.

Source C: From an interview with the manager of an aircraft factory, by the Listener Research Section of the BBC.

'I approve very strongly of the broadcast about the **dog-fight** in the Channel last Sunday which has created much interest. I feel that it acted as a real tonic to many people and gave them something to talk about. It created a much more healthy atmosphere than the wild rumours which are commonly discussed. There is no denying that people will talk, so give them something good to talk about.'

'There is great interest in the sensational running commentary by Charles Gardner on Sunday on the air fight he watched over the English Channel. Many were enthusiastic about the broadcast. However, he included phrases such as 'Oh boy, oh boy, this is the best thing I've seen', as young men were crashing to their death, to which some viewers took exception.'

'Having personally witnessed fighting at first hand and seen people killed, I disapprove of the broadcast by Charles Gardner which has caused me much discomfort and some nausea. There is little doubt that a certain section of the population will be stimulated by a broadcast of this type. However, the description, of brave men going to their doom did not appeal to me at all and was in bad taste.'

Agreement

Source B agrees that some people were enthusiastic about the broadcast. Source A says that it acted as a real tonic to the people and Source C suggests that some people were stimulated by the broadcast.

Disagreement

There is also disagreement between the sources. Source A strongly approves of the broadcast whilst the writer of Source C strongly disapproves.

Films

Films were another important method of keeping up morale. The cinema was a popular form of entertainment. Between 25 and 30 million tickets were sold every week in Britain. Many of the audience went to the cinema to escape from the hardships of war-time life. The Ministry of Information brought out documentaries – such as 'Fires were Started', which was about London during the Blitz – and encouraged the British cinema industry to produce films which entertained cinemagoers but also kept up morale and increased support for the war effort.

In addition, propaganda films were shown in the workplace at lunchtime to boost both the morale of workers and their production rate.

Activity

2. Here is another example of a cross-referencing question for you to look at.

   How far do Sources D, E and F suggest that propaganda films kept up morale?

Source E: A photograph taken in 1940, during the Battle of Britain, of a crowd of people in the street watching about the battle. This is being shown by a mobile film unit.

> This photograph cannot tell us how people reacted generally. It only shows one event and we do not know how representative it is of the time.

Source D: From the diary of Elsie Whiteman who worked in an aircraft factory in Croydon, June 1941.

> Source D should be reliable, because the writer will have written her genuine views of the film in the diary.

'At dinner time today the Ministry of Information film "Let's Finish the Job" was shown in the canteen. It was a really wonderful film. It was very cleverly devised. The rights and wrongs of doing jobs was shown in an amusing way. The moral was, that how we finish the job is very important.'

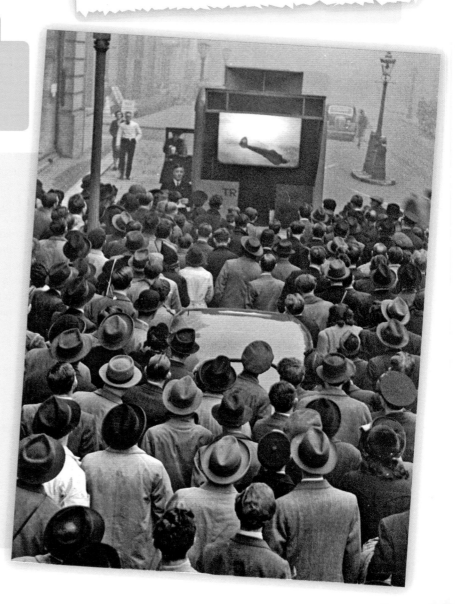

52

Helping hand

Once again, begin by examining the content of the three sources. Highlight or annotate the sources in different colours.

- Green to show where details in the sources support the view.
- Red where details of the sources challenge the view.

One example has been done for you for Source F. The next stage is to examine the reliability of the source to see how reliable each source is in supporting or challenging the view. Once again

- Green to show where nature and origins of the sources strengthen the view. See the example for Source D.
- Red to show where nature and origins of the sources weaken the view. See the example for Source E.

Source F: From an interview given by Phyllis Warner in 2001 for a book on the Home Front during the Second World War.

'I remember going to see *Target for Tonight* in August 1941, a new film of a bombing raid on Germany in which all the actors were members of Bomber Command. It was a memorable film. At first my sympathies were with the German anti-aircraft gunners on the ground. However, this soon changed to sympathy for our airmen on their lonely and perilous journey back to Britain. There was something about their simple cheerfulness.'

Did you know?

During the Second World War, German radio made propaganda broadcasts to Britain. By January 1940, six million were listening to the most popular ones by 'Lord Haw-Haw', the nickname of William Joyce – who was later executed by the British for treason, even though he was an American citizen.

Activity

3. How reliable is Source F as evidence of the importance of propaganda films? In your answer remember to:
   - Compare the information given in the source to what you know.
   - Check the Nature, Origins and Purpose of the source. Does it exaggerate? Is it one-sided?

4. On the home front during the Second World War, in what ways did the government use the following?

   a) The radio.

   b) Films and the cinema.

5. Make a final judgement on the question:

   How far do Sources D, E and F suggest that propaganda films kept up morale?

   Make a copy of the scales below.

   - On the left hand side put all the evidence supporting the view from the three sources, including details and reliability.
   - On the right hand side put all the evidence challenging the view from the three sources, including details and reliability.

6. Overall, what is the conclusion to your answer?

Making a judgement

Government propaganda often gave the British people an exaggerated – even distorted – view of what was going on. Sometimes it even told lies. If you were a member of the Minister of Information during the Second World War, what arguments would you use to defend such propaganda?

Utility

2.4 Immediate reactions to the NHS

Lesson objectives

By the end of this lesson, you should be able to:
- understand why, at first, the medical profession opposed the National Health Service
- understand how to evaluate the **utility** of a source, using its content and nature, origins and purpose.

One key skill is the ability to evaluate the usefulness and limitations of a source or sources. This could be written sources such as letters, diaries, speeches or images, including cartoons, photographs or posters. You are going to evaluate the utility of sources in the context of immediate reactions to the NHS.

Introducing the NHS

In 1946 the National Health Act was passed, and two years later, on 5 July 1948, the National Health Service began, and was welcomed by most people. However, it at first faced powerful opposition from the medical profession, especially doctors.

Activity

1. You may be asked to decide the usefulness of a source or sources. For example:

   How useful is Source A as evidence of reasons for the introduction of the NHS?

Helping hand

Every source will have strengths and weaknesses. Therefore, your answer should reflect this by explaining the usefulness and limitations of the contents and the Nature, Origins and Purpose of the source. Here we will concentrate on the usefulness and limitations of the contents of Source A.

Source A: From a speech by Aneurin Bevan in 1946 introducing the National Health Act. Bevan was Minister of Health in the Labour government, which had won the General Election of 1945 partly because of its promise to set up the NHS.

Medical treatment should be made available to rich and poor alike in accordance with medical need and no other criteria. Worry about money in a time of sickness is a serious hindrance to recovery. The records show that it is a mother in the average family who suffers the most from the absence of a full health service. In trying to balance her budget she puts her own needs last. A proper health service must ensure that the rich and poor are treated the same.

Bevan does not mention that one of the main reasons for the introduction of the NHS was the promise to set up a health service made by the Labour Party in the General Election of 1945.

Useful, because it suggests some of the reasons for the introduction of the NHS, such as medical treatment for all, even those with little money.

Bevan mentions the important reasons for the NHS and illustrates this with evidence of how poorer families suffered before its introduction.

Opposition from the medical profession

There was strong opposition to the introduction of the NHS from the British Medical Association (BMA). The medical profession feared that they would lose their independence, waste valuable time filling in forms and have their earnings controlled by the government.

In January 1948, the BMA held a **ballot** of all its doctors to see whether they approved of joining the NHS. Over 40,000 voted against the NHS Act, with just 4,700 supporting it.

Activity

2. Try to answer the following questions about the contents of Source A.
   - What is useful about what it suggests?
   - From your own knowledge, how accurate is the view it expresses?
   - Does it give fair or balanced coverage of the topic? Are there any key views or factors which are missing? If so, is this deliberately done?

Source B: From an article in the *British Medical Journal*, January 1946.

If the National Health Service Bill is passed, no doctor or patient will feel safe from interference by some member of the government or by some regulation. The Minister of Health's spies will be everywhere. The Bill also threatens the independence of the general practitioners who will become government servants.

Nature of source
This is useful, because the journal would reflect the views of many doctors who opposed the new NHS.

Origins of source
Useful because it was at the time when there was strong opposition from doctors to the National Health Act.

Purpose of source
Its usefulness is limited because of its purpose, which is to turn people against the NHS and force Bevan to make changes. Therefore, it deliberately exaggerates the negative effects of the National Health Act for doctors.

Origins of source
It is written in a doctor's journal which will give a very one-sided view of the National Health Act. It only mentions the bad effects of a NHS and uses strong language such as 'spies'.

Activity

3. Give two reasons why many doctors opposed the National Health Act.

4. Answer the following question about Source B using its NOP:
   How useful is Source B as evidence of why doctors opposed the NHS?

Helping hand

To evaluate a source, also think about the usefulness of the Nature, Origins and Purpose (NOP) of the source. Look at Section 2.2 for further guidance on these, but remember that in Section 2.2 you analysed the purpose of sources.
- What is useful about the Nature, Origins and Purpose of the source?
- What are the limitations of the Nature, Origins and Purpose of the source?

You do not have to examine all three of these attributes, as long as you evaluate at least one of them.

Glossary

ballot: a vote done in secret

utility: usefulness

56

Source C: A cartoon from the *Daily Mail*, May 1946. It shows the votes for and against the introduction of the NHS. The figure on the left is the secretary of the BMA.

The purpose of the cartoon is to encourage support for the NHS and turn the public against the BMA. Therefore, the newspaper deliberately exaggerates reactions to the NHS.

Useful because it was a cartoon produced at the time when the National Health Service was introduced. It was published in a popular newspaper which was trying to reflect the popularity of the NHS.

The cartoonist deliberately shows a massive pile of voting papers in support of the NHS which towers over those that oppose it. This is useful, because it suggests that there was strong support for the introduction of the NHS.

Only a few votes shown in opposition to the NHS. The secretary of the BMA is shown as being overwhelmed by the votes in favour. This suggests there was little opposition to the NHS from the public.

It is a cartoon trying to make a point, and will exaggerate reactions to the NHS – shown by the huge pile in support, and the very small number against.

Hill meets mountain!

Bevan gives way

Bevan eventually had to give way to the BMA. He allowed consultants to work within the NHS and at the same time treat private patients and earn high fees. In May 1948 opposition from the BMA crumbled and when the NHS was finally introduced in July 1948, 90 per cent of doctors had enrolled.

Immediate effects

At first, people rushed to have free eye and dental treatment, many having neglected their eyes and teeth for years because of the cost. In the first year alone, eight and half million people received dental treatment and over five million pairs of glasses were provided.

The government had estimated that the NHS would cost about £176 million a year. However, costs had reached nearly £400 million per year by 1949.

Helping hand

You will also need to evaluate the usefulness of the contents and Nature, Origins and Purpose of illustrations. Here it is important to closely examine the information given about the source as well as the details shown in the illustration.

Activity

5. What can you learn about the NHS from Source D?

6. Study Source E. How useful is this source as evidence of the effects of the National Health Service? Copy and complete the following grid to help you plan your answer.

	Usefulness	Limitations
Contents		
Nature, Origins, Purpose		

Helping hand

Remember that you do not have to evaluate all three – Nature, Origins and Purpose. For example, you could evaluate just the Origins of Source D, as has been done below.

Making a judgement

In order to persuade doctors – especially consultants – to accept the new National Health Act, Bevan agreed that they could have private patients. Do you agree that there should be private patients who have to pay for their treatment, alongside a free National Health Service?

Source D: From an interview with an 83-year-old woman in 1995, who remembered the start of the NHS.

Useful

From an interview given nearly fifty years later with a woman who actually experienced the early NHS and was able to reflect on its achievements.

When the National Health Service came in it was much easier to see a doctor, and it was free! My teeth had been bad since I had a baby and I was now able to have false teeth at no cost. They were sore at first but soon bedded in and became comfortable. Some of my friends got teeth because they were free but never used them. My mum got free spectacles and we noticed how much better she could see.

Limitation

The interview was given many years later by an 83-year-old woman whose memory of some of the details may have faded.

Source E: From a cartoon published in the *Daily Express*, December 1949.

"Dentist says if there are any more of you thinking of fitting one another up with National Health teeth for Christmas presents you've had it."

Testing a hypothesis

58

2.5 Civilians in the firing line: the Blitz

Lesson objectives

By the end of this lesson, you should be able to:
- understand how people reacted to the **Blitz**
- use sources to test a **hypothesis**.

By a hypothesis we mean a view of a given event or person. Historians base their own views on a range of sources they have consulted. You are going to use a range of sources to test a hypothesis in the context of how people reacted to the Blitz of 1940-41. As you saw in Section 1.6, British civilians have been in the firing line on several occasions during the 20th and early 21st centuries, including the First and Second World Wars, the IRA campaign and, more recently, the London bombings of 7 July 2005.

Key features of the Blitz

From September 1940 to May 1941, the Germans bombed the centre of British towns and cities in what became known as the Blitz. The main aim was to force the British to surrender by destroying the **morale** of the British people by targeting their homes.

Every major town and city, including Coventry, Liverpool, Plymouth and Manchester, was bombed, with over two million homes destroyed and 43,000 people killed. London was the primary target, especially the East End with its docks, factories and crowded terraced streets. For example, between 2 September and the 2 November 1940, London was bombed every night.

The hypothesis

You are going to test the following hypothesis:

'*The Blitz of 1940-41 did not destroy the morale of the British people*'.

This is a popular hypothesis about the Blitz.

Activity

1. Note down which elements of Source A support the hypothesis. One element has already been highlighted for you.

Source A: From an article in the *Evening Standard*, January 1941.

'Seventeen women and children who were trapped in the basement of a London house damaged by a bomb last night, shouted to **wardens** who went to their rescue: "We're all right. Look after everybody else". Then they all started singing "Tipperary" and shouting to the people in the road. "Are we downhearted? No".'

Support

Source A strongly supports the view. The whole tone of the article suggests the 'Blitz spirit'. Even though their house has been damaged, they are singing and seem cheerful.

Source B: A photograph published in a London newspaper in November 1940. It shows a family that refused to leave their home and protected it with sandbags.

HOME SWEET HOME

Activity

2. Now look at Sources B and C to see if they support or challenge the hypothesis.

   Remember to examine the contents of each source. You will need to apply your inference skills to understand what the sources are suggesting. Copy and complete the following grid to record your answers for all three sources (A-C).

Source	Support	Challenge

Source C: Extract from a government report into the effects of bombing of Portsmouth, January 1941.

'By 6.00 pm all traffic is moving northwards. The movement begins at 3.30 pm and continues to dusk. The people are making for the bridge on the main road out of Portsmouth in order to sleep in the northern suburbs, the surrounding hills, or towns and villages in the radius of twenty miles. One night it was estimated that 90,000 people left the city. Looting and wanton destruction have reached almost alarming proportions. The effect on morale is bad and there is a general feeling of desperation.'

The 'Blitz spirit'

One view is that Blitz did not lower the morale of the British people, but actually had the opposite effect. It created the 'Blitz spirit' making people even more determined to support the war. Newspapers and radio broadcasts lost no opportunity to portray the Nazis as evil. Everyone remained cheerful and seemed even more determined to resist Hitler. For example, the London Underground was fully of jolly singing as people sheltered from the bombs. When Buckingham Palace was bombed, the Queen said she was glad because it meant she was sharing the experiences of many Londoners, especially in the East End.

In addition the Blitz did less damage than many people had expected. It did not greatly reduce the production of factories. Furthermore, damage to transport was quickly repaired.

Glossary

Blitz: the German bombing of British cities

the establishment: people at the top of society or the people in control

hypothesis: a viewpoint or idea

looting: stealing goods from homes and shops during a general crisis

morale: mood, how positive you feel

wardens: civilians with special duties during an air raid

Other views of the Blitz

However, there is some evidence that not everyone agreed with the 'Blitz Spirit' and that the Blitz did damage civilian morale.

60

- Some people in the East End of London, which suffered the worst of the bombing, complained that members of the government, in the less threatened West End, did not do enough to help the homeless.

- Coventry was hit by 30,000 bombs on one November night and the city centre was almost destroyed. People were so terrified that they fled the city and slept with relatives or in farmers' barns.

- In Portsmouth, which was badly bombed in January 1941, as many as 90,000 fled the city and there was evidence of looting.

- In Britain nearly three million homes were destroyed during the Blitz

- Britain suffered more civilian than military casualties. Over 40,000 people were killed and many were made homeless

Helping hand

'The Blitz of 1940-41 did not destroy the morale of the British people'.

Does Source D support or challenge this view?

This question is asking you to test the hypothesis by using Source D. To do this you will need to:

- examine whether the contents support or challenge the statement

- now evaluate the reliability of the source in supporting or challenging the statement. Remember to evaluate the reliability of the information it gives as well as the Nature, Origins and Purpose.

Activity

3. Evaluate the reliability of Source D. Remember when evaluating reliability

   - Compare the information given in the source to what you know.

   - Check the Nature, Origins and Purpose of the Source. Does it exaggerate? Is it one-sided?

Source D: From a German radio report, 18 September 1940

Content

Source D strongly challenges the view. The whole tone of the article suggests that the Blitz has destroyed the morale of the British people, who are panicking and losing all discipline and self-control.

'The legend of British self-control and coolness under fire is being destroyed. All reports from London agree in stating that the people are seized by fear – hair-raising fear. The 7 million Londoners have completely lost their self-control. They run aimlessly about the streets and are victims of bombs and bursting shells.'

Reliability

This challenge is weakened by the reliability of the source. This is because it is from a German radio report with the purpose of illustrating the success of the Blitz in destroying the morale of the British people, and will exaggerate its effects.

Activity

4. Now evaluate the reliability of Sources E and F to see if they support or challenge the hypothesis.

   Remember to examine the Nature, Origins or Purpose and contents of each source. You will need to apply your inference skills to understand what the sources are suggesting.

5. Copy and complete the following grid for Sources D, E and F.

Source	Support or challenge	
	Reliability	Contents

Activity

6. Study Source B. What was the purpose of this photograph?

7. Study Source E. What is the message of this cartoon? How does the cartoonist put across this message?

8. Working in pairs study Source D. Put together a brief BBC radio report responding to this German broadcast.

Source E:
A cartoon from the London Evening News, September 1940. The caption reads 'Well I must be toddling in now. I mustn't miss the 9 o'clock news'.

Source F: From a history of the Second World War, published in 2007.

'There was [a] darker side to the so-called Blitz Spirit. Looting was rife. Records show 10,000 people were prosecuted nationwide and traders in London claimed they lost more through looting than by bomb damage. Nor was everyone always in it together. Members of **the establishment** were able to take refuge in country houses or in expensive basement clubs in the City while lower, middle and working classes were forced to remain in cities and face up to the deadly raids with inadequate shelters.'

Helping hand

'The Blitz of 1940-41 did not destroy the morale of the British people'.

How far do Sources A-F support this statement?

In this question you are being asked to make a final decision on the hypothesis based upon the evidence given in all six sources.

Which question?

At GCSE level, the type of question you will answer will depend on what GCSE specification you are taking.

- Type A questions will ask you to test a hypothesis using **5** sources and contextual information.

- Type B questions will ask you to test a hypothesis using **3** sources and extra information of your own.

There now follows aan opportunity to practise both types of question.

Activity

9. Copy and complete the grid below, making a judgement on the strength of evidence given by each source based on its provenance and contents. Use a scale of 1-5 for each source with 5 being strong evidence and 1 being very weak evidence.

	Supporting the view (1-5)	Challenging the view (1-5)
Source A		
Source B		
Source C		
Source D		
Source E		
Source F		
Total		

10. Now use the information in your grid to make a final judgement on the hypothesis based on the strength of evidence supporting or challenging the view.

Helping hand

'The Blitz of 1940-41 did not destroy the morale of the British people.'

How far do you agree with this statement? Use your own knowledge, Sources A, B and D and any other sources you find helpful to explain your answer.

This question is similar to the previous question in certain ways.

- You have to examine the contents of Sources A, B and D to determine whether they support or challenge the hypothesis. Remember that you have already done this for the first hypothesis using your grid.

- You have to evaluate the reliability of the three sources to determine whether they support or challenge the hypothesis - remember to consider the NOP of the three sources.

- However in addition, you should make use of any other knowledge about the effects of the Blitz to either support or challenge this hypothesis.

- The examples of the 'Blitz Spirit' on page 59 could be used to support the hypothesis. For example the Blitz seemed to have the opposite effect and rather than destroying morale, seemed to make people even more determined to support the war.

- You may, if you wish, make use of other sources such as Source E, but remember to examine its contents and evaluate its reliability as well.

- To challenge the hypothesis use examples from page 60, such as in Portsmouth where as many as 90,000 fled the city and there was evidence of looting.

Finally, think about the strength of the evidence of the sources. Make a comment if the evidence is particularly strong or weak.

Did you know?

On the night of 29 December 1940, hundreds of bombs were dropped on the area of London round the cathedral of St Paul's. A famous photograph published in national newspapers showed that the only building that was not damaged was St Paul's, with the exception of the High Altar. Many saw this as a miracle, and a symbol of the 'Blitz Spirit'.

Activity

11. Copy and complete the following planning grid for the following hypothesis

    'The Blitz of 1940-41 did not destroy the morale of the British people.'

    How far do you agree with this statement? Use your own knowledge, Sources A, B and D and any other sources you find helpful to explain your answer

    Use the information in the Helping Hand box to help you fill in your grid.

	Score (1-5)			
	Support	**Challenge**	**Reliability**	**Strength**
Source A				
Source B				
Source D				
Own knowledge				
Another source or sources				

12. What is your final judgement on this hypothesis based on the weight of evidence?

    - in Sources A, B, D and any other sources you used
    - your own knowledge

Making a judgement

The Blitz caused considerable damage to the centre of many towns and cities but did not succeed in destroying the morale of the civilians. Do you think this was due simply to very good government propaganda, which created the 'Blitz Spirit'?

Analysing and evaluating representations

3 The trenches and trench warfare

Lesson objectives

By the end of this lesson, you should be able to:

- understand what is meant by representations of history
- analyse representations
- compare how far they differ
- evaluate representations.

A representation means how someone has depicted something in the past – possibly an event or an individual – visually or in words. Historians, novelists, cartoonists, film-makers and painters give us their view or image of the past. In this section you will learn how to analyse, evaluate and compare different representations of the **trenches** and trench warfare.

The historical context

Much of the fighting during the First World War took place in an area between Belgium, France and Germany known as the Western Front. Here, at the end of 1914, the two sides – Britain and France, against Germany – dug trenches. For the next three years, there was trench warfare, with neither side able to break through.

The soldiers on both sides lived in the trenches, where conditions were often very unpleasant, unhygienic and dangerous. Much of the fighting took place in an area between the trench system known as **no-man's-land**. Here, many soldiers were killed or wounded as they tried to advance on the enemy trenches. This trench warfare was condemned at the time and in later years, because of the terrible conditions and the many thousands who were killed.

For example, on the first day of the Battle of the Somme, 1 July 1916, nearly 60,000 British soldiers were killed or wounded attacking German trenches. In the following year, British attacks during the Third Battle of Ypres got bogged down in very muddy conditions in no-man's-land, leading to even heavier casualties. The use of new weapons such as poisonous gas made the conditions worse and caused even more casualties.

However, research does suggest that some soldiers enjoyed the comradeship and humour of life in the trenches. Trench warfare created unique, deep and long-lasting friendships. Moreover, some soldiers were only too pleased to put up with the hardships and suffering of the trenches for the sake of **patriotism** – to serve their country.

Helping hand

When analysing an artist's representation of the past, you should examine carefully what is shown, and ask yourself the following questions:

- What has the person who created the representation selected, or chosen to show? Pick out details from the source.
- What has the person who created the representation omitted to show? Give examples.
- How was the scene portrayed? Give examples.
- What message is given by the representation?

Source A: '*The Harvest of Battle*', a painting by C R W Nevinson, in 1919.

Notice the deliberate choice of words in the title of the painting, '*Harvest of Battle*', to give the impression of many casualties rather than of military gain.

Sky shown as grey and overcast. Water shown as dull green and dirty.

No-man's-land – shown as a barren, horrible place with **shell-holes**, pools of water and no trees or buildings. There are fragments of barbed wire.

Many dead bodies shown in no-man's-land. Several men have been wounded and are being helped by other soldiers. One soldier is being carried on a stretcher.

There is still fighting going on, with evidence of explosions and fires in the background.

The overall message or view of Source A is that trench warfare was horrific, barbaric and awful. In order to put across this message, the artist has deliberately selected a particular scene from trench warfare: no-man's-land, which shows the dead and the wounded as well as explosions. No-man's-land itself is depicted as a barren wasteland with shell-holes and pieces of barbed wire.

Moreover, the artist has used specific, depressing colours, to reinforce the message, and has made no attempt to show daily life in the trenches themselves, or the friendship and camaraderie between the soldiers.

Glossary

no-man's-land: the area between the two trench systems which became a wasteland due to constant shelling by both sides

patriotism: a love of, and devotion to your country

shell-holes: huge craters in no-man's-land caused by the constant artillery fire by both sides. These craters were often full of water

trenches: zig-zag defensive positions dug by both sides. By 1916, the Germans had three – in some places even four – lines of trenches

66

Source B: A modern historian's view of the First World War from 2011.

There were two sides to trench warfare. On one side, there were the dangers from enemy bombardment which brought injury and death, as well shell-shock caused by the constant strain of living under shellfire. On the other side there were strong feelings of friendship and comradeship between the soldiers which helped them to share the dangers in the trenches. They didn't want to let their mates down. This comradeship was also reinforced by feelings of patriotism as they were fighting for their home and country. Many soldiers had a sense of playing their part in a historic event and were surprised by what they found they could achieve. In addition there was much humour in the trenches as it provided a release from the dangerous and unpleasant conditions. One such example can be seen in the cartoon shown opposite. This was drawn by a British officer on the Western Front, Bruce Bainsfather. His cartoons of trench life were very popular with the troops as well as being published in the British media. He showed many situations from trench life in a light-hearted and humorous way.

Most of the account is about the positive side of life in the trenches, especially comradeship and patriotism.

Further evidence of positive side of trench life and warfare, with reference to humour and cartoons. The historian has deliberately selected and used a humorous cartoon.

Cartoon shows in a humorous way, the togetherness of the men in the trenches, with one soldier pouring a drink for another, and a soldier playing the accordion.

Notice the deliberate choice of words by the historian, to give a more positive image of trench warfare.

In and Out (II)

That first half-hour after "coming out" of those same trenches

Helping hand

In analysing written representations, use the same skills you applied to the illustration:

- What has the person who created the representation selected or chosen to write about? Pick out details from the source, especially the words used.
- What has the person who created the representation omitted to write about? Give examples.
- What message is given by the representation?

An example of this has been done above for Source B.

Source B is written by a historian. They write their own representations of the past, by choosing what to concentrate on. Most of Source B focuses on the positive side, as well as the humour. The historian reinforces this more optimistic view by the choice of the cartoon. The writer also creates this message with a careful choice of words such as 'comradeship', 'togetherness', 'patriotism'.

However, historians do try to give a more balanced view of the past. For example, the account does mention death and injury, although, the overall message is that there was a positive side to trench warfare – especially the friendships that were created.

Helping hand

You will be asked to compare two representations. For example, Sources A and B are both representations of trench warfare. How far do they differ?

- Ensure you have analysed each representation.
- What is the main view or message of each source, about trench warfare?
- What similarities or differences are there in their view or message?
- How has each representation put across this message? Use details from each source.
- Finally, make a judgement about how much difference there is between the two representations. Use judgement words or phrases, such as, *strongly agree, strongly disagree, slightly agree, slightly disagree*.

Here are some examples of similarities between the two representations:

Source A	Depicts the horrors of trench warfare by showing dead and wounded in no-man's-land
Source B	Historian also mentions such horrors with smashed bodies and wrecked trenches

Here are some differences:

Source A	The artist had deliberately chosen a horrible scene in no-man's-land to give a very bleak, negative view of trench warfare
Source B	The historian gives a more balanced view but, overall, has also deliberately chosen examples of the positive side of trench warfare, including the humorous cartoon.

Source C: From the novel *All Quiet on the Western Front*, published in 1929. It was written by Eric Remarque, a German soldier who experienced life in the trenches from 1917–18.

'We were eighteen and had begun to love life and the world; and we had to shoot it to pieces. Bombardment, barrage, curtain-mines, gas, tanks, machine-guns, hand-grenades – words, words, words, but they hold the horror of the world. I am young yet I know nothing of life but despair, death, fear, suspended over a deep chasm of sorrow. Trenches, hospitals, the common grave – there are no other possibilities.'

Activity

1. Analyse Source C, as a representation of trench warfare.
- Examine carefully the words or phrases chosen by the author.
- What is the overall message of the source?

Helping hand

You will also have to evaluate a representation. This means deciding how good it is using your own contextual knowledge. You can do this by asking three questions of each representation:

- Does the representation give an *accurate* view compared to your own contextual knowledge?
- Does it give a *complete* view compared to your own contextual knowledge? Is anything missing?
- Does it give an *objective* view? This means balanced, and not favouring one side or the other. Here, the purpose of the author or artist will help.

Now let's do this by looking at Source A again.

Source A: '*The Harvest of Battle*', a painting by C R W Nevinson in 1919.

This is a very one-sided view of trench warfare. The artist does not give a *complete* view of other trench warfare. The painting does not show the more positive aspects of daily life in the trenches, more especially the humour or friendship.

This is not an *objective* view of trench warfare, because the artist exaggerates its negative features in order to emphasise the futility of trench warfare.

This is an *accurate* representation of trench warfare: there were many casualties in no-man's-land – as shown in the painting – an example being on the first day of the Battle of the Somme in 1916.

Activity

2. Explain another difference in Sources A and B as representations of trench warfare.

3. Which statement best sums up the differences between Sources A and B as representations of trench warfare?
   - There are strong differences
   - There are some differences
   - There are few differences.

4. Which do you think is the better representation of trench warfare, Source A, Source B or Source C? Make a copy of the following table to plan your answer. Give a brief comment on each source in each section, and rate each source on a scale of 1–5, with 5 being the highest for each question. Some examples have been done for you.

Making a judgement

You have now completed your planning table for Sources A, B and C. In your judgement, which source gives the best representation of trench warfare? State your reasons.

	Accuracy (1–5)	Coverage (1–5)	Objectivity (1–5)
Source A	**4** Gives an accurate view of the casualties in no-man's-land such as during the Battle of the Somme.		
Source B			**4** The purpose of the historian is to give an objective, balanced view of trench warfare.
Source C		**1** Does not mention any of the positive features of trench warfare – friendship and patriotism	

Enquiry skills

Carrying out an historical enquiry

Lesson objectives

By the end of this lesson, you should be able to:
- select and organise your material for an enquiry
- write up your enquiry.

In this section you will see how to carry out research for an enquiry, and write it up using the following flow diagram. You will use these skills in the next two sections.

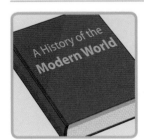

1 Finding out what the enquiry is about

The first stage is to identify what the enquiry is about.

- What is the topic area of the enquiry? For example, in the next section it is the Cuban Missile Crisis, and the section after that, the Holocaust.

- What is the precise question? Is it asking you to write about causes, consequence, change or significance? You will have to research a causation question on the Cuban Missile Crisis and a change question on the Holocaust.

2 Getting a basic outline

Start with a general textbook, in order to get a basic outline of the topic. This could be three or four pages from a general history of the period. For the Cuban Missile Crisis or the Holocaust, this could be a history textbook. Begin to organise these notes into smaller headings such as causes, events and results. Ensure that you make a note of the book title, author, and the pages where you found the information.

3 Finding out more detail

You can now extend your research to include more detailed resources such as chapters of a textbook. On Cuba, this could be textbooks on the Cold War or International Relations, and on the Holocaust it could be histories of Germany for the period. Your research should also include actual sources such as letters, diaries, speeches, cartoons and television documentaries. For example, on Cuba and the Holocaust, there are several useful documentaries. Again, ensure that you make a note of any book title and author, and the pages where you found the information.

4 Finding these resources?

Your teacher will give you help and guidance, but some examples are school textbooks, the school or local library, and the Internet.

5 Sorting out relevant information

This is an important skill. Do not make notes on every feature of the topic. Be selective. Choose what is relevant to the enquiry question. For example, the enquiry in the next section is about the events of the Cuban Missile Crisis, so although you will find information about why the crisis happened, your more detailed research and note-taking should be on why it ended peacefully. Similarly, on the Holocaust, you will find information on Nazi policies towards the Jews before 1939, but focus your detailed research on 1939 and after.

6 Checking for reliability

Be careful when using resources, especially Internet data, which are sometimes anonymous, and may contain opinions, but with no factual support. Check the reliability of actual sources by applying your Nature, Origins and Purpose skills. Do not discard unreliable – especially one-sided – sources; they can provide one view of the event.

7 Carrying out further research

You may well have identified further key features of your enquiry question and need to carry out more research. For example, the exchange of letters between the two leaders during the Cuban Missile Crisis, or details of the Wannsee Conference, which led to the 'Final Solution' in the Holocaust.

8 Planning your answer

Having carried out your research and collected relevant information, you now have to organise this information, in order to answer the specific enquiry question. You could summarise your key points in a concept map, drawing arrows to show how the factors link. On the other hand, you could make use of a planning grid such as the one here.

Introduction	Sets the scene
First factor	Identified and explained Linked to second factor
Second factor	Identified and explained Linked to third factor
Third factor	Identified and explained Linked to conclusion
Conclusion	Your final judgement

9 Coming to a conclusion

Finally, you need to make a judgement on the enquiry question. If the question is causation – such as the Cuban Missile Crisis enquiry – you need to decide which was the most important reason and be able to justify your choice. If the question is change – such as the Holocaust enquiry – you need to focus on how much change there was.

Carrying out an enquiry

4.1 The Cuban Missile Crisis

Lesson objectives

By the end of this lesson, you should be able to:
* understand how to carry out an enquiry
* select and organise your material on the Cuban Missile Crisis.

The Cuban Missile Crisis was the most serious crisis of the **Cold War** with the two superpowers, the USA and the USSR, close to nuclear war. Your enquiry focus is on the crisis itself

Why was the Cuban Missile Crisis of 1962 settled peacefully?

Remember that you studied causation in section 1.1. This should help you in answering this enquiry question.

Background to the Cuban Missile Crisis

The crisis was due to two main developments: the Cold War between the USA and the USSR, and changes in Cuba.

In the years after 1945, rivalry increased between the USA and the USSR. This rivalry became known as the Cold War. The USA was determined to prevent the spread of **communism** by the USSR. Both countries took part in an **arms race**, developing ever more powerful nuclear weapons of mass destruction.

Helping hand

First you will need knowledge and understanding of the background to the Cuban Missile Crisis, especially what led to the crisis itself. You need to think about what may or may not be relevant to the enquiry question.

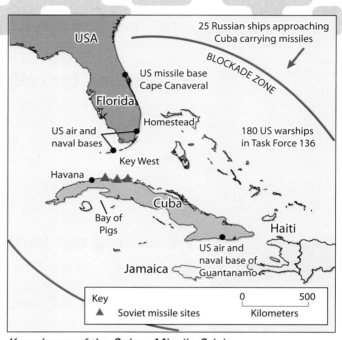

Key places of the Cuban Missile Crisis

Cuba is an island very close to mainland USA. In 1959 Fidel Castro led a successful revolution against the military ruler of Cuba – General Batista, who had been very much under the influence of America. Castro removed American influence from Cuba and moved closer to the USSR. In 1961, the USA organised a failed attempt – known as the Bay of Pigs invasion – to overthrow Castro.

Castro grew closer to the **Soviet** leader, Khrushchev and, in May 1962, agreed to station Soviet nuclear weapons on Cuba. On 14 October an American U-2 spy plane took photos revealing that missile sites were being built on Cuba.

Activity

1. Which of the following, if any, are directly relevant to this research question?
   * Castro's takeover
   * The Bay of Pigs invasion
   * The discovery of the missile sites.

Helping hand

The previous section, pages 68–69, gave you advice on how to carry out your enquiry. Now you need to start selecting information that is relevant to your enquiry question. Remember that the focus of your enquiry is why the crisis ended peacefully. It is about causation, so you are trying to find reasons.

The beginning of the crisis

On Tuesday 16 October, US President John Kennedy was informed of the discovery of the missile sites. Kennedy assembled a group of experts and colleagues known as the Ex Comm committee to decide what action to take. He had four options:

Option	Likely outcome
Do nothing	This would avoid war but would make Kennedy and the USA seem weak.
Attack Cuba with nuclear weapons	This could lead to nuclear retaliation against the USA from the USSR.
Attack Cuba with conventional weapons, e.g. using air strikes	This attack could kill Soviet soldiers and engineers and lead to the outbreak of war with the USSR.
A naval **blockade** of Cuba to stop Soviet ships delivering missiles to Cuba	This would not be a direct act of war and would put the responsibility on Khrushchev as to what to do next. However, it would not solve the main problem – the removal of the missile sites on Cuba.

Helping hand

You now need to select any reasons during the crisis, that brought about a peaceful ending. For example: out of the options available to Kennedy, which one was

- most likely to lead to war
- least likely to lead to war?

If you think you have found a relevant reason, you may wish to carry out further research on Kennedy's options. Most modern world textbooks should include a section on the crisis. You could also consult internet sites, but be careful because not all of these are reliable. Remember to make a note of the title and author of any books or other resources you use.

Activity

2. Put together a flow chart showing the key events of the Cuban Missile Crisis. Here is a start for you.

> **16 October**
> **Kennedy is informed of the Soviet missile sites on Cuba**
> ↓
>

3. You will end up with a summary of the key events of the crisis. However, not all these events will be relevant to your enquiry question. Highlight in one colour any key features which will help you answer the enquiry question.

Glossary

arms race: competition between the USSR and the USA to develop the most advanced weapons of mass destruction

blockade: surround and block the entry or exit from a place

Cold War: the stand-off or state of hostility between the USA and the USSR in the years 1945-91 which fell short of actual war

Soviet: a term used to describe something or someone from the USSR.

Communism: belief in a classless society where all private ownership is abolished

superpowers: the two most powerful countries in the world after 1945

Kennedy's actions

Kennedy decided on a naval blockade of Cuba which would prevent further missiles and equipment reaching Cuba. He announced his decision in a televised speech made on 22 October, and the following day the blockade was set up.

The attitude of Khrushchev

Khrushchev insisted that the Soviet government was simply helping Cuba to defend itself and that the USA was interfering in Cuba's affairs. He accused the USA of pushing the world towards nuclear war.

The crisis reached its height on 25 October, as 25 Soviet ships sailed closer to Cuba. The USA and the USSR were ready to use their nuclear weapons. Then suddenly the Soviet ships stopped. One oil tanker was allowed through unsearched and the rest turned back. One American politician said: 'We were eyeball to eyeball and the other side just blinked.'

Source A: An extract from Kennedy's televised speech, 22 October 1962.

'We will not needlessly risk world-wide nuclear war in which even victory would be ashes in our mouths – but neither will we shrink from that risk when it must be faced . . . I call upon Chairman Khrushchev to stop and dismantle this secret, reckless and provocative threat to world peace.'

Helping hand

Remember that you are now trying to identify specific reasons why the crisis ended peacefully, which should include the attitude of Khrushchev.

- Ensure you can explain why Khrushchev's attitude was important.
- You may wish to carry out further research on Khrushchev's attitude. Remember to make a note of the title and author of any books or other resources you use.

Source B: A British cartoon of 29 October. It shows Kennedy (on the right) and Khrushchev arm-wrestling for power, sitting on nuclear weapons. The caption says: 'OK Mr President, let's talk'.

This is only a one-sided view of the crisis, and suggests that Khrushchev is the one who is backing down. It is from a British cartoonist – the British were close friends of the USA.

The cartoon also suggests that Khrushchev was prepared to open talks to try to find a peaceful solution.

The cartoon shows the serious nature of the crisis by showing an arm-wrestling contest between the two leaders, who are sitting on nuclear weapons.

Helping hand

Sources can provide useful information relevant to your enquiry question. However, you need to:

- summarise key points relevant to your enquiry question
- evaluate the reliability of each source. Look at the example for Source B on page 74.

Activity

4. What can you learn from Source A about the crisis?
5. Does the source give a reliable view of the crisis?

Exchange of letters

On the 26 October, Kennedy received the first letter from Khrushchev. This suggested that the USSR would withdraw the missile sites from Cuba, if the USA promised not to invade Cuba. Khrushchev finished the letter by highlighting the possibility of nuclear war.

On the following day, the 27 October, the Soviet leader sent a second letter which changed his conditions for removing the missiles from Cuba. The USA would, in return, have to remove missiles from Turkey – which bordered the USSR. On the same day, an American U-2 spy plane was shot down over Cuba with the pilot killed. Kennedy was advised to launch an immediate attack on Cuba. Once again the world was on the brink of nuclear war.

The crisis ends

However, Kennedy decided to delay such an attack and, instead, responded to Khrushchev's first letter. The US president insisted that if the missiles were not withdrawn from Cuba, then the USA would attack.

Source C: Khrushchev's letter to Kennedy, 28 October.

'In order to eliminate as rapidly as possible the conflict which endangers the peace, the Soviet Government has given a new order to dismantle the arms which you described as offensive and to crate and return them to the Soviet Union.'

Helping hand

The exchange of letters between the two leaders is another important factor in answering your enquiry question.

- Be clear you understand and can explain why.
- You may wish to carry out further research on these letters. Remember to make a note of the title and author of any books or other resources you use.

Helping hand

You should now be able to identify several reasons for your enquiry question. Remember, you will not be asked to simply describe these factors, but to explain why they brought about a peaceful solution.

Activity

1. Summarise the main reasons why the Cuban Missile Crisis was settled peacefully. You could use
   - bullet points
   - a mind map
   - sketches.

Making a judgement

Both Khrushchev and Kennedy played important roles in bringing about a peaceful solution to the crisis. Which leader do you think played the more important role? Give reasons for your judgement.

Writing up your enquiry

4.2 The Cuban Missile Crisis

Lesson objectives

By the end of this lesson, you should be able to:
- plan your enquiry answer
- write a focused and structured answer.

A very good enquiry essay:

- focuses on the question
- uses information from different resources/ sources
- backs up all statements with information
- is well organised and structured
- communicates clearly using good spelling, punctuation and grammar.

Understanding the enquiry question

Why was the Cuban Missile Crisis of 1962 settled peacefully?

Be clear about what the question is asking. You could underline or highlight key words in the question.

- '*Why*' means the focus is on causation, i.e. reasons. Do not just tell the story, describe or narrate what happened, answer the question.
- '*Cuban Missile Crisis*'. The question is about the crisis itself, not its causes and consequences.
- '*settled peacefully*'. The focus is on why it did not lead to war.

Introduction

You should begin your essay with an introduction. The introduction:

- sets the scene for the enquiry question
- suggests the main factors you will explain.

Example 1

In 1959 Fidel Castro overthrew Batista and became the leader of Cuba. He got rid of the influence of the USA on the island and became closer to the communist Soviet Union. America decided to get rid of Castro but the Bay of Pigs invasion was a failure. In October 1962, a US spy plane discovered that the Soviet Union was building missile sites on Cuba.

Example 2

On 14 October 1962, a US spy plane took photographs of Soviet missile bases on the island of Cuba. This discovery sparked off a crisis which lasted for thirteen days and brought the world very close to nuclear war. However, the crisis was eventually settled peacefully due to the actions and decisions taken by President Kennedy of the US, and the Soviet leader, Khrushchev

Activity

1. Look at the two example introductions.
   - Which would be the more effective?
   - Why?

Focused paragraphs

Each of the paragraphs in the body of your essay should fully focus on answering the question.

- The first sentence should directly refer to the answer to the question – in this case, the reason the crisis was settled peacefully.

- Most of the rest of the first paragraph should explain this factor.

- The paragraph conclusion should make a judgement on the importance of this factor.

Here is an example of this three part paragraph.

> One reason why the Cuban Missile Crisis was settled peacefully was because of Kennedy's decision to blockade Cuba.
>
> When Kennedy was informed about the presence of Soviet Missiles on Cuba, he was faced with three.........
>
> This was a very important reason for the peaceful solution to the crisis because if he had chosen the ....

Activity

2. Before you begin writing up your answer, put together a mind map summarising the main reasons why the Cuban Missile Crisis was settled peacefully. Draw lines showing links between some of these reasons. Write these link details along the lines. An example has been done for you.

Making links

You should try to make links between one paragraph (one factor) and the next. For example if you write a paragraph on Kennedy's decision to impose a blockade on Cuba, you could link this to Khrushchev's subsequent decision to order the Soviet ships to turn back. Here are some useful link words and phrases:

Moreover, however, as a result of, consequently, therefore, this led to, this resulted in.

Reference to resources/sources

You should have kept a record of all the resources and sources you have consulted, including those from the Internet. Ensure that you make reference to these in your essay, including those you have used from pages 72–75 of this textbook.

One method for this is to:

- put together a list of resources/sources you have consulted, including the title, author and page references.

- number each resource

- place these numbers in your essay where you have referred to these resources/sources.

Here is an example of a bibliography:

1. Walsh, B., *Modern World History*, pages 347–51

2. Waugh, S., *Essential Modern World History*, pages 274–78

3. Bunce, R., Gallagher, L., and Kelly, N., *History A: The Making of the Modern World*, pages 100–107

4. www.spartacus.schoolnet.co.uk/coldcubanmissile.htm

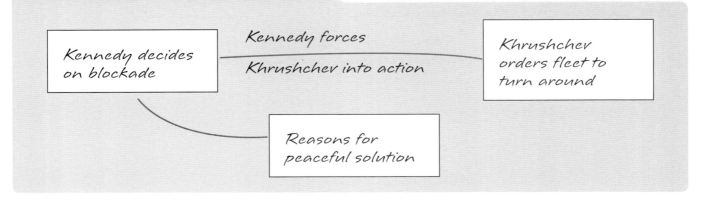

Activity

3. Read example 3. Working in pairs, how could you improve this answer? Remember:
   - three-part paragraph
   - focus on the question
   - links
   - resource/source references.

Example 3

On the 26 October Kennedy received a long letter from Khrushchev. In the letter, the Soviet leader claimed that the missiles on Cuba were purely defensive. He also offered a deal: 'If assurances were given that the USA would not participate in the attack on Cuba and the naval blockade was lifted, then the Soviet Union would remove the missiles'. The next day, Khrushchev sent a second letter saying that he would only remove the missiles if the USA did the same in Turkey.

Kennedy replied to the first letter in which he said that if the Soviet Union did not withdraw, he would attack.

Conclusion

You now need a strong conclusion. Remember, this is the last part of your essay to be assessed. It should:

- reinforce the links between the factors
- make a judgement on the relative importance of the factors. For example: Which do you think was the most important factor? Why was it more important than the others?

Example 4

The Cuban Missile Crisis ended on 28th October. Kennedy and Khrushchev had managed to come up with a deal in which the Soviet Union withdrew the missiles from Cuba and the USA promised not to attack the island. The two leaders later set up a hot-line between the White House and the Kremlin.

Activity

Read example 4 above.

4. How could you improve this conclusion?
5. Reorganise the mind map you did earlier. Rank-order the importance of each reason, beginning with the most important at 12 o'clock and working your way clockwise.
6. On your mind map, explain why the reason you placed at 12 o'clock is more important than the others.

Most important

Least important

Reasons for peaceful solution

Second in importance

Planning your essay

You are now ready to plan your answer. Here is a
planning grid to help you. Remember to include
only what is relevant to the enquiry and to directly
refer to any sources you have used. You may wish
to explain more than three reasons.

Introduction	Set the scene: What is the enquiry about and what are the main factors you will explain.
First reason	Give the reason, and fully explain it. Remember to make reference to resources/sources used. Try to make a link to the second reason.
Second reason	Give the reason and fully explain it. Remember to make reference to resources/sources used. Try to make a link to the third reason.
Third reason	Give the reason and fully explain it. Remember to make reference to resources/sources used. Try to make a link to the next reason.
Conclusion	Which do you think was the most important reason? Why is it more important than the others. Explain your answer.

Carrying out an enquiry

4.3 The Holocaust

Lesson objectives

By the end of this lesson, you should be able to:
- understand how to carry out an enquiry
- select and organise your material on the Holocaust.

The Holocaust was the deliberate murder of over six million Jews in Europe between 1933–1945 by the Nazi Party. Your enquiry focus is on how Nazi policy towards the Jews changed in the years after 1939:

How much change was there in Nazi policies towards the Jews in the years 1939–45?

Remember that you studied change in section 1.5.

Background information

Hitler hated the Jews and had used them as the **scapegoat** for Germany's problems after the First World War. He regarded them as inferior, and was determined to remove them from Germany.

Hitler became Chancellor of Germany in January 1933, and in the years that followed gradually stepped up his campaign against Jews in Germany. The campaign included:

- boycotting Jewish shops and businesses

- banning Jews from top professions, such as solicitors, doctors, dentists and accountants

- banning them from public places, such as parks and swimming baths

- depriving them of German citizenship.

The campaign against the Jews really stepped up after the events of *Kristallnacht* which means the Night of the Broken Glass, 9–10 November 1938. The **SS** organised attacks on Jewish shops, with over 815 destroyed and many synagogues set on fire. Nearly 100 Jews were killed and a further 20,000 arrested and sent to **concentration camps**.

In January 1939, Reinhard Heydrich, one of the leaders of the SS, was given the task of eliminating the Jews from Germany. This would be achieved by forced emigration. The Nazis wanted other countries to take the Jews as refugees, and even discussed a scheme to settle Jews on the island of Madagascar, off the coast of Africa.

Helping hand

Pages 70–71, gave you advice on how to carry out an enquiry.

This enquiry is about changes in Nazi policies after 1939. However, to look at change, you must first understand what the situation was in 1939 and compare it to what followed.

You will need to summarise information relevant to your enquiry question.

Activity

1. What changes took place in Nazi policy in the years 1938–9? Are these changes relevant to your enquiry question?

The Second World War

The first year of the Second World War (1939–40), brought changes in Nazi policies towards the Jews. The advancing German armies occupied Poland, where three million Jews lived.

- The Nazis now had to deal with many more Jews outside of Germany itself.

- Forced emigration was no longer a realistic policy. There was simply nowhere to send so many Jews.

The Nazis had to come up with more drastic solutions to what they saw as the 'Jewish problem'.

Activity

2. Using the following table, make a note of any changes in Nazi policies towards the Jews. One example has been partly completed for you.

Change and date	Actions	Attitudes	Numbers affected	Amount of suffering
1939	Forced emigration		All Jews in Germany	

The Ghettos

The SS rounded up the Jews from country and town areas all over the new German Empire and moved them into ghettos. These were in the slum areas of the major cities, surrounded by high walls and armed security guards.

Source A: From a speech in 1940 by Richard Heydrich, the head of the **Gestapo**, about the setting up of ghettos.

'The first step for the final aim is the concentration of the Jews from the countryside into the larger cities.'

The Nazis established at least 1,000 ghettos in German controlled Poland and the Soviet Union alone. The largest ghetto in Poland was the Warsaw ghetto, where over 400,000 Jews were crowded into an area of 1.3 square miles.

The Germans regarded the establishment of ghettos as a temporary measure – to control and keep Jews separate from non-Jews, until the Nazis decided on a more long term solution.

Helping hand

To show change you should make comparisons using words such as: more / less, before / after.

Source B: From *The Holocaust, The Jewish Tragedy*, M Gilbert, 1987.

This should provide a reliable view of this change in Nazi policy as it was written by an historian who should give an objective and balanced view.

'On 3 October, 1940, the German Governor of Warsaw announced that all Jews living outside the mainly Jewish district would have to leave their homes and move to the Jewish area. Warsaw was to be divided into three areas: one for Germans, one for Poles, and one for Jews. The Jews, who were one-third of the population, were to move into an area less than two and a half per cent the size of the total city.'

The source gives details of how ghettos were organised in Warsaw, and suggests that the Jews were forced to live in very overcrowded conditions.

Glossary

concentration camps: prisons where inmates were treated with great brutality

Gestapo: the Nazi secret police

SS: the organisation that removed opposition to the Nazis

scapegoat: someone who is blamed for, and punished for the errors of others

Source C: A photograph of Jewish families being arrested by Nazi troops in the Warsaw ghetto in 1943.

Conditions in the ghettos

People were taken away and never heard of again. The conditions in the ghettos were appalling, with many dying from starvation and disease. Rations were deliberately tiny. Many Jews were also worked to death. Groups of forced labourers were taken under armed guard to work on building projects where they could be beaten if they stopped work.

Helping hand

The focus of your enquiry is on changes in Nazi policies towards the Jews. The use of ghettos was a significant change in Nazi policy, so should be included in your table.

You may wish to carry out further research on this change in policy. Remember to make a note of the title and author of any books or other resources you use. You will find that most textbooks on Nazi Germany will include at least one section on the Holocaust.

You could also consult internet sites but be careful because not all these are reliable or appropriate.

Activity

3. Are the conditions in the ghettos relevant to the enquiry task? Do these show change?

4. What can you learn from Sources A and C about the ghettos?

5. Do they give a reliable view of the ghettos?

The *Einsatzgruppen*

In June 1941 the Germans invaded the Soviet Union and, by the end of that year, had occupied huge areas of the west of the USSR, in which there were millions of Jews. This worsened the 'Jewish' situation, and the Nazis brought in a temporary solution: the *Einsatzgruppen*, or special murder squads.

These squads moved into Russia behind the advancing German armies to round up and kill Jews. By 1943 it was estimated that the squads had murdered more than one million Russian Jews.

Source D: A statement by the head of *Einsatzgruppe D* at his trial in 1946.

'The Einsatzgruppen were carrying out orders. They would enter a village or a city and order the prominent Jewish citizens to call their people together for the purpose of resettlement. They were requested to hand over their valuables to the leader of the unit, and shortly before execution, to surrender their outer clothing. The men, women and children were led to a place of execution which in most cases was located next to a deeply excavated anti-tank ditch. Then they were shot kneeling or standing, and the corpses thrown into the ditch.'

Helping hand

The *Einsatzgruppen* were another change in Nazi policy towards the Jews. You need to add this change to your table and summarise the key changes. You may wish to carry out further research on this change in policy. Remember to make a note of the title and author of any books or other resources you use.

Activity

6. What can you learn from Source D about the activities of the murder squads?

7. How reliable is this source?

The 'Final Solution'

This was the name given to the Nazi policy of killing all Jews in German-occupied areas of Europe. In the summer of 1941, due to the massive numbers of Jews now under Nazi control, leading Nazis such as Goering and Himmler began to seek a permanent and efficient solution to the Jewish problem.

Source E: Auschwitz Commandant Rudolf Hoess writing in 1959.

'In the summer of 1941, I cannot remember the exact date, Himmler received me and said in effect: 'the Fuhrer has ordered that the Jewish question be solved once and for all. The Jews are the sworn enemies of the German people and must be eradicated. Every Jew that we can lay our hands on is to be destroyed now during the war, without exception. If we cannot obliterate the biological basis of Jewry, the Jews will one day destroy the German people.'

A meeting of leading Nazis at Wannsee, near Berlin, in January 1942, worked out the details of the 'Final Solution'.

- Death camps were to be built in Poland.

- Jews would be rounded up and transported by train to these camps where some would be worked to death.

- Those not able to work would be killed in gas chambers.

Work was carried out very quickly on the construction of these camps – which included gas chambers and crematoria – at places such as Auschwitz and Treblinka. The first death camp at Belzec began operating in March 1942, and by the summer of 1942 Jews from all over Europe were being transported to these camps.

84

Source F: David Mekler, an eyewitness, describes how Jews were rounded up from the ghetto in the Polish town of Lodz and sent to Belzec.

'On 11 April 1942, the SS and mounted police fell like a pack of savages on the Jewish quarter. It was a complete surprise. Our community then numbered ten thousand. In no time at all, without even realising what was happening, a crowd of about three thousand men, women and children were driven to the station and deported to an unknown destination. The scene in the ghetto after the attack was horrible. Bodies everywhere, in the streets, in the courtyards, inside the houses. Babies thrown from the third or fourth floors lay crushed on the pavements.'

Activity

7. What can you learn from Sources E (on page 83) and F (above) about the Final Solution?

8. Do the sources give a reliable view?

Helping hand

The 'Final Solution' is another change in Nazi policy.

- Add this to your table and ensure that you can explain how this changed Nazi policy towards the Jews.

- You may wish to carry out further research on this change. Remember to make a note of the title and author of any books or other resources you use.

A map of the sites of Nazi death camps in Poland.

The death camps

On arrival at the death camps, the Jews were divided into two groups:

- Those who were fit were put to work. They were worked to death in the labour camps. There was a strict daily routine, with roll-calls for several hours per day prior to forced labour in mines or factories. The conditions were terrible and they were given very little food, consisting of just bread and thin soup. Disease spread quickly.

- The others were sent to the gas chambers. Older women, mothers with children and children under ten were usually taken immediately to be executed in the gas chambers. There was little opposition because most gas chambers were fitted out as showers, so that the prisoners would not realise what was happening to them. Bodies were burnt in ovens or left in mass burial pits.

By the time the camps were liberated by the Allies in 1945, six million Jews had been worked to death, gassed or shot.

Source G: Roll-call at Auschwitz I on a Christmas Eve. This was painted by a camp prisoner after the war was over.

Helping hand

The death camps are another change in Nazi policy.

- Add this to your table and ensure that you can explain how this changed Nazi policy towards the Jews.
- You may wish to carry out further research on this change. Remember to make a note of the title and author of any books or other resources you use.

Activity

9. What can you learn about the death camps from the map on page 82 and Source G?

10. Put together a time line summarising the key developments in Nazi policy towards the Jews in the years 1939–45. Here is a start for you. Indicate in the last column whether this was a change or continuity. For example, did the Nazi attitude to the Jews change during this period?

Date	Policy	Change or continuity
1939	Reich Central Office for Jewish Emigration	Continuity in hatred of Jews but definite change in method

The Nuremberg Trials

Twenty two of the Holocaust leaders were put on trial at Nuremberg in 1946. A new charge of 'crimes against humanity' was introduced to deal with the Holocaust. Nineteen men were found guilty, with twelve of these being executed. There were many eye-witnesses and – because the Nazis had been very efficient in their record-keeping – enormous amounts of detailed evidence of how the Final Solution worked. This helped to prove the extent of the guilt.

Helping hand

Are the Nuremberg trials relevant to your enquiry?
If so, summarise their main features.

Making a judgement

In 1938, Jewish shops and synagogues in Germany were attacked and destroyed by the Nazis. By 1945 over six million Jews in Europe had died at the hands of the Nazis. Which Nazi policy brought the most change?

Writing up your enquiry

4.4 The Holocaust

Lesson objectives

By the end of this lesson, you should be able to:
- plan your enquiry answer
- write a focused and structured answer.

In this enquiry you should find out about each of the developments in the timeline and how they made a change to the lives of Jews in Germany:

1939	The introduction of Ghettoes
1941	The *Einstatzgruppen*
1942	The Wannsee Conference and the Final Solution
1942–45	The death camps

Understanding the enquiry question

Be clear about what the question is asking. You could underline or highlight key words in the question as has been done here:

How much did Nazi policies towards the Jews change in the years 1939-45?

- The focus of this question is 'change'. Do not just tell the story, describe or narrate what happened but write about change. Use change words such as *more, less, different, increased, worsened*

- 'Nazi policies towards the Jews'. The question is about changes in how the Nazis dealt with the Jews.

- '1939-45'. The question is about Nazi policies in these years only. .

Introduction

You should begin your essay with an introduction. This

- sets the scene for the enquiry question

- suggests the main changes you will explain.

Activity

1. Look at the two example introductions below.
   - Which would be the more effective?
   - Why?

Example Introduction 1

> In 1939 the Nazis set up ghettos for Jews in towns in cities. Then in 1941 they organised murder squads known as the Einsatzgruppen. In the next year the Nazi leaders met at Wannsee and decided on the 'Final Solution'. They set up death camps.

Example Introduction 2

> In the years after 1939, the number of Jews under Nazi control greatly increased as German armies expanded eastwards into Poland and the Soviet Union. In response to this, Nazis policies towards the Jews changed from the introduction of ghettos in 1939 to the decision to carry out the 'Final Solution' two years later

Focused paragraphs

Each of the paragraphs in the body of your essay should fully focus on answering the question.

- The first sentence should directly refer to the question. For example give the change.

- Most of the rest of the paragraph should give details which support this change.

- The final part should make a judgement on the change.

Here is an example of this three part paragraph.

> One change in Nazi policy was the setting up of ghettos in major towns and cities in the years 1939–41. This meant great changes to the lives of many Jews compared to beforehand. These changes included........
> The importance of the change was.......

Making links

You should try to make links between one paragraph (one factor) and the next. For example if you write a paragraph on the Wannsee Conference you could link this to the setting up of the death camps.

Helping hand

Here are some useful words and phrases you can use to link text:

Moreover; however; as a result of; consequently; therefore; this led to; this resulted in.

Activity

2. Put together a mind map summarising the main changes in Nazi policies towards the Jews in the years 1939–45.

   Draw lines showing links between some of these changes. Write these links along the lines. Here is a start for you –

Changes

Decision taken to introduce new policy 'The Final Solution', which needed...

Wansee Conference

Death camps

Reference to resources/sources

You should have kept a record of all the resources and sources you have consulted, including those from the internet. Ensure that you make reference to these in your essay including those you have used from pages 80–85 of this textbook.

One method is to:

- Put together a list of resources/sources you have consulted, including the title, author and page references

- Number each resource.

- Place these numbers in your essay where you have referred to these resources/sources.

Here is an example of a bibliography:

> Child, J. Germany 1918–39
> Waugh, S. Life in Germany
> www.het.org.uk

Conclusion

You now need a strong conclusion. Remember this is the last part of your essay to be assessed. It should make judgements on

- how much change there was in the years 1939–45

- what was the most important change.

Activity

3. Look at the example conclusion below. How would you improve this example?
   Example conclusion

Example conclusion

> The Nazis introduced different policies towards the Jews. In Germany they were persecuted. In areas occupied by the German armies they were herded into ghettos, killed by murder squads or sent to death camps. In 1946, 22 of the Holocaust leaders were put on trial and found guilty of crimes against humanity.

Glossary keywords

3d three pennies in pre-decimal currency (the same price as a loaf of bread)

absolutist conscientious objector who refused to do any military duties including non-fighting duties

a just cause a reason for doing something that is morally right

anonymously acting without giving your name

arms race competition between the USSR and the USA to develop the most advanced weapons of mass destruction

ballot a vote done in secret

blackout stopping any lights showing after dark, so enemy bombers couldn't tell where the towns and cities were

Blitz the German bombing of British cities

blockade surround and block the entry or exit from a place

cause something you believe in and want to make happen

coalition an alliance of different countries that is not permanent, but made for one particular action

Cold War the stand-off or state of hostility between the USA and the USSR in the years 1945-91 which fell short of actual war

communism belief in a classless society where all private ownership is abolished

concentration camps prisons where inmates were treated with great brutality

conscription making people join the army

dog-fight a battle in the air between aircraft

evacuees children sent out of the cities (which the government feared would be bombed) to the countryside

Gestapo the Nazi secret police

hypothesis a viewpoint or idea

infectious easily passed from one person to another by touch or breath

join up join the military services of a country

looting stealing goods from homes and shops during a general crisis

media ways of mass communication

militant someone prepared to use extreme methods to get what they want

morale mood, how positive you feel

mortality rate the number of people in certain categories (e.g., age groups, region they live in) who die

munitions weapons of various sorts

nationalise when the state takes over the running of an industry

neutral a neutral country is one that has stated it will not get involved in the wars of other countries, on any side

no-man's-land the area between the two trench systems which became a wasteland due to constant shelling by both sides

patriotism a love of, and devotion to your country

propaganda public information given to people to affect the way they think and behave

public health services services that improve the general health of everyone in the country: such as mains drainage, rubbish removal, clean water

Quaker a member of a religious group, known as the Society of Friends

rationing restricting how much of certain foods or other goods each person can buy

scapegoat someone who is blamed for, and punished for the errors of others

shell-holes huge craters in no-man's land caused by the constant shelling by both sides. These craters were often full of water

Soviet a term used to describe someone or something from the USSR

SS the organisation that removed opposition to the Nazis

suffragette the nickname given to members of the WSPU, who were prepared to use extreme methods to get the vote for women

suffragist someone who believed in peaceful methods of campaigning for the vote for women

superpowers the two most powerful countries in the world after 1945

the establishment people at the top; people in control

trenches zig-zag defensive positions dug by both sides. By 1916, the Germans had three – in some places even four – lines of trenches

unemployment benefit a weekly amount paid by the state to people qualifying for the payment and who cannot find work

utility usefulness

Western Front area of the trench system in France and Belgium where most of the fighting took place during the First World War